Copyright © 2020 David K

ISBN: 979-8868348556 (Paperback)

Any references to historical events, real people, or real places are used fictitiously. Names, characters, and places are products of the author's imagination.

Front cover image by David Kasneci.
Book design by David Kasneci.

Printed by Palmetto Publishing, Alpha Graphics, Metro Webb, Bind-Rite in the United States of America.

First printing edition 2022.

David Kasneci
243 Broadway #9188 SMB #11120
Newark, NJ 7104.

www.369project.com

DISCLAIMER

THE CONTENT OF THIS BOOK IS FOR INFORMATION AND EDUCATIONAL PURPOSES ONLY. Nothing in this book constitutes professional and/or financial advice, nor does any information in the book constitute a comprehensive or complete statement of the matters discussed or the law relating thereto. Project 369 is not a fiduciary by virtue of any person's use of or access to the Site or Content. The content herein is not financial advice. This book may offer information regarding living a wealthy, prosperous, and abundant life (including, without limitation, information concerning self-realization exercises, affirmation exercises, meditative brain wave state exercises), but such information is intended for educational and informational purposes only. Neither the author nor publisher makes any representations as to the safety of the practices set forth in this book. Please consult a licensed medical professional and or a licensed financial advisor if you have questions or concerns. The practices discussed in this book should not be taken as medical, health, or financial advice.

Table of Contents

Table of Contents

Acknowledgments

I would like to express my deepest gratitude to all of those who have been with us since day one of Project 369—Those who have discovered the power within themselves to create and manifest anything they want into their lives.

I express my deepest gratitude to the inspirational teachings of Neville Goddard, Napoleon Hill, Dr. Joseph Murphy, Esther Hicks, Wayne Dyer, Earl Nightingale, Alan Watts, Dr. Joe Dispenza, James Allen, Bob Proctor, Joseph Rodrigues, Dolores Cannon, and William Walker Atkinson.

I am both humbled and grateful for Stephen Sainato for being a world-class coach, Alex Charafeddine for his ability to transform individuals and teach sales at a profound level, Rosey Kasneci for loving me, and Orjor Kasneci for giving me a new life.

I am thankful for my family, who has made me the person I am today, while also guiding me through love, acknowledgment, and compassion.

Last but not least, I am blessed and cannot be more appreciative of my team at Project 369 for their dedication to serving the awakening.

Introduction

Those who have created abundance, prosperity, and wealth all have one thing in common: they all obtain a Wealth Consciousness. Wealth Consciousness is the state of consciousness or mind that every prosperous and wealthy individual has cultivated and manifested. It is this very state of consciousness that I will endeavor to cultivate within you by the end of this book.

For all who know Project 369, you know that our books are not mere books; they are all workbooks that recondition your mind through scripting practices and deep esoteric knowledge not known to the average individual but by means created for the average individual to understand. Project 369 is a transformative journey that will change your life... if you allow it to.

Within these pages, we'll dive deep into understanding what Wealth Consciousness is and how you can harness it to not only improve your financial standing but elevate every aspect and quality of your life in every conceivable dimension. I aim to create a shift in your perspective from seeing wealth as something external that you may be chasing after to something internal, dormant, and ready to be awakened and manifested.

Although this book is targeted toward those who desire to create financial freedom and prosperity, obtaining a Wealth

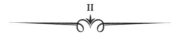

Introduction

Consciousness does not only guide you in accumulating money, a Wealth Consciousness manifests abundance in all forms. Money, as you'll come to understand, is not just a physical currency. It's an energetic exchange, a reflection of value, and a manifestation of your relationship with abundance, just as everything else you receive from the world.

Money is not something that is only for those who are born rich people, or those whose circumstances deem it possible, or those who just got lucky, oh no, no. Money is for you. It is your birthright. It is something that has been screaming your name. It is something that you must obtain and something you will obtain. It is something that is necessary for you to create a happy, fulfilled, and grateful life.

Many have been led to believe that in order to make money, we must work extremely hard for it. We are led to believe in the illusion of hard work. While conscious effort is necessary to do anything you have not yet done, I aim to show you the path of least effort, least energy, and least resistance, where things that you thought would be hard gradually become effortless with a shift in mental attitude and perspective.

We will be exploring the very essence of your being – the "I AM." This is not the ego or personality-based 'I' that you often refer to

Introduction

as "me" and associate with your identity, but the infinite, all-powerful, and all-knowing Unconditioned Creator that lies within you, beyond the "me." Within I AM is contained every potential and possibility that could ever exist. I AM is the center and core of your very existence. When we tap into the infinite I AM beyond the "me," we tap into the root of abundance and the wellspring of boundless prosperity, the true wealth we never knew existed within the illusion of the ego.

This workbook consists of 3 parts: (1) Shadow Work and Letting Go, (2) Reprogramming and Auto-Suggestion, and (3) Effortless Action and Cosmic Will.

In part one, you will dive into the subconscious shadow and uncover hidden barriers, fears, and limiting beliefs that have held you back from truly embracing and creating wealth and prosperity. Alongside, you will reveal the hidden powers and qualities of abundance and wealth that may have been neglected and suppressed by reason of fear.

In part two, you will reprogram your subconscious mind through daily autosuggestion, affirmations, and exercises. You will do this for 30 consecutive days to ensure success in reprogramming and reconditioning old limiting beliefs with new ones. You will also learn powerful techniques that will aid you in attracting wealth.

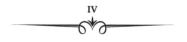

Introduction

In part 3, you will come across the final stage of cultivating a Wealth Consciousness, which is the training of your will and the expressing of your newly reconditioned Wealth Consciousness. I endeavor to teach you how to unlock a Cosmic Will that is beyond your will, and perform effortless action toward your goals and aims of creating prosperity.

After reading and finishing the workbook, you should have cultivated a Wealth consciousness and should be expressing it effortlessly. However, Wealth Consciousness is a state that must be nurtured, taken care of, and trained throughout the entirety of our lives. In the same way that our state changes throughout the days, weeks, months, and years, so will our state of consciousness. It is up to you to continue to evolve and reach higher states in your journey toward prosperity, for no one will do so for you, as you are the one and only Creator.

It is up to you to accept the knowledge contained within this book. I encourage you to read this book habitually, over and over again, so the concepts and truths can stick in your mind so that you can evolve your perspective toward money and prosperity, and so you can gradually reach higher states and planes of the Wealth Consciousness. I speak from experience when I tell you: *the very moment you choose to commit to obtaining a wealth consciousness will be the very moment you become wealthy.*

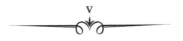

Balance

Before we dive into living a prosperous, wealthy, and abundant life, I want to emphasize that no matter how much you desire to live a prosperous life, you should never make money your primary goal and forget to include a balanced life.

Abundance is your birthright, and your desire for abundance should include not only an abundance of material wealth, but also an abundance of perfect health, purpose, love, peace, happiness, and joy. You never want to get to a point where money is the only thing that gets your attention, and you lose sight of everything else you are here to experience.

Money is merely a medium of exchange; money is nothing more than energy. Through an increase in your attention and a change in your beliefs, you can surely attract all the money you desire, but relying on money for your happiness and keeping all of your attention on money alone can lead you to build a not-so-friendly relationship with money.

If you only want money in this life, you will not be satisfied. Again, you should not only desire money, but you should desire all of the beauty life has to offer. By relying on money and focusing only on riches and material wealth, you may find yourself saying, "My life has been ruined by money. As a result, I've lost love, I'm perpetually unhappy, I'm unhealthy, and I'm lost."

"For the love of money is the root of all evil." Indeed, it is, and it will continue to be for as long as one loves money more than anything else.

Balance

You see, it is not money itself that is evil. A belief like this will never get you closer to money. As a matter of fact, it will just push you further away from it. Money is only evil for those who are controlled by it.

In truth, evil is anything that controls you. Evil is anything external you rely upon for happiness, peace, love, and satisfaction.

Both the rich and the poor can be controlled by money. The poor may need it; the rich may not be satisfied. If so, the poor lack abundance, and the rich lack gratitude. You may think your current position in your outer world dictates how much money you can make, but in truth, it is your inner world that dictates it.

When man realizes that he is forever projecting his inner world, and his outer world is forever reflecting what he is projecting, only then will he be able to find the true cause, which will forever be his mental state or state of consciousness. Man is forever conditioning his consciousness by changing his beliefs, and the day man changes what he believes to be true is the day man changes his entire world.

Your beliefs create all of your experiences. Your life is but the reflection of all you believe to be true about yourself and your world. Take a moment now and ask yourself what you believe to be true about money. Do you believe money is evil? Do you believe only people who sell drugs or do illegal things can have the most money? Do you believe there is not enough money to go around? Do you believe that you can make as much money as you could possibly desire?

Service

The amount of money you can make is directly correlated to the amount of value you can provide. If you provide great value, you will make great money. The more skillful you become, the more value you can provide, and the more value you provide, the more money you will make.

The journey of having a prosperous life begins with asking, "How can I serve others? What can I serve? Who can I serve?" Lastly, after you find the answers to those questions, you come to the biggest question of all, which is, "Why am I serving?" Surprisingly, not many ask this question. Instead, people only ask questions like, "How can I make money? What can I make money with? Who can give me money?"

There is no problem whatsoever with figuring out how to make money. This is something you need to figure out, no matter what. However, in order for you to figure it out, you must not only think of serving yourself, you must think mostly about serving others. If you only think of ways you can make money, you may never find the one to make you the amount of money you want, and you may never find the one that puts a smile on your face and makes you happy, and you may never find the one that you love to do and get rewarded for doing it.

Now, let's say you think of ways you can make the world a better place, and you are focusing on serving others. In this instance, you will have more than enough money, and you will be more than happy and satisfied as a result of serving others. Love and Abundance will flow as a result of the love you are extending through your service to others.

Transformation

All transformation occurs through a burning desire. If you have no desire to be transformed, there will be no transformation, and your life will continue to be as it is. Transformation can only occur through a change of consciousness, and a change of consciousness can only occur through a change in belief. If you believe you are perfectly fine, and you don't need to change anything, there will be no reason for you to change, and it will be practically impossible for you to build a burning desire to change.

At every moment that passes, you are creating and manifesting your life through your state of consciousness, or state of mind. With this realization, know that you hold the power to create and manifest anything into your life simply by entering and expressing a new state. You see, every potential and possibility exists here and now, regardless of whether or not you currently think of them as possible, and once you choose to enter a new state, life will reflect it.

In order to get what you desire, you must be ready to receive it. Therefore, ask yourself, "Do I have the same thought patterns, emotions, and behaviors as I would if my desire were here right now?" If your answer is yes, you are on the right track. If not, you can change them by cultivating a burning desire to change. If you were ever to change yourself and create a life you truly desire, you must realize that you are the only creator, and there is no external cause that will aid you or do it for you. Therefore, make the decision now to tap into the infinite storehouse of desire power within, and create yourself and your world as you truly desire.

The Universe Is Mental

Your mind is like a radio. When you tune your radio to a country station, you will get country music. When you tune your radio to a hip-hop station, you will get hip-hop music. Similarly, when you tune your mind to abundance, you will receive abundance, and when you tune your mind to lack, you will receive lack. Your mind is a radio tuned by you, forever giving you that which your station is tuned to.

You see, everything physical and nonphysical in the Universe is comprised of energy, frequency, and vibration. You channel energy through your attention, and tune your frequency to a certain station through the thoughts you feel and accept as true.

If your frequency is tuned to prosperous and abundant thoughts, your station will provide you with harmonious, abundant thoughts. If your frequency is tuned to worry and fear-based thoughts, your station will provide you with harmonious worry and fear-based thoughts.

You are an infinite creator, creating yourself and your life through the gifts of speech and mind. You have the power to tune your frequency to any station you desire, thus being anyone you desire to be. Choose thoughts and words that are in harmony with your vision and dreams. Focus your attention and tune your frequency on the station you desire, for you cannot be tuned to two stations at the same time.

Within the Universal Mind of the Unconditioned Creator is contained every possibility and potential that could ever exist. In other words, any station you could possibly think of tuning into exists and can be

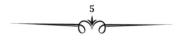

The Universe Is Mental

accessed by tuning your frequency to the thoughts, feelings, and behaviors contained within that station, respectively. Once you successfully tune your frequency to the correct station, there will be no option but for you to express it and sing along to the tunes of abundance. for what is impressed must always be expressed.

You see, where and how we tune our frequency doesn't just affect the thoughts we are receiving from the according station. Most of your behaviors and emotions are also influenced, and varying on the degree of influence, controlled by the station you are tuned to. What stops many of us from tuning our frequency to a different station is the station we're currently on. We are so used to hearing the same thoughts that we don't want to change them at all, even if they are harmful in nature. Many times, we believe the station we're tuned to is the only station that exists, and this is because it is the only station we know, so we identify with that station and call it our unique station.

In truth, we did not choose the station currently playing in our heads. This station has been tuned since birth by the people who raised us, the places we were raised in, and the things we were raised with. When we were kids, we didn't know right from wrong or good from bad. We accepted everything we were taught as true of ourselves and our world.

So then, our station was tuned not by us; it was tuned by the world. If we are not taught that we have the power to tune our frequency to any station we desire, then we will believe the station we're in is the only station that is real and true, and the only station that exists.

The Universe Is Mental

You, my friend, are not the station you are tuned to. You are the one tuning your station. Awaken to the realization that within you is contained every station that could possibly exist, and all you must do is cultivate a burning desire to be on the station you prefer and believe it is possible for you to tune your frequency to it. I tell you now that I know it is possible, for I speak from experience when I say that anything is possible to those who want hard enough and those who believe.

Begin now. Tune your frequency to the station you desire by thinking thoughts in harmony with the one you desire to be and feel and accept these thoughts as true of yourself and your world. Tell nobody your doings, for they only see and know the evidence of the station they have tuned themselves to.

Know that, in truth, you are far greater than you think you are, and it is time for you to realize this truth for yourself.

Know that, in truth, all experiences in this life are neutral, and you are given the power and free will to create every single one of your experiences through your divine perspective.

Know that, therefore, a change in perspective is a change in your entire experience of life as you know it to be currently.

Know that, in truth, it is not the world that you must change, but self, for there is nothing to change but self in this world.

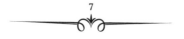

The Illusion of Hard Work

Many of us have been told that those who make millions and even billions of dollars have done so solely through hard work, effort, sweat, tears, and tremendous labor. You are told that if you do not work hard in this life, you will not make much money or be successful.

I will tell you now that this concept of working very hard for money is an illusion. Even the concept most people hold of hard work alone is an illusion. Hard work, most if not all of the time, is merely a concept used to describe concentrated attention. He who has found the storehouse of infinite and divine willpower and desire power within knows there is no such thing as hard work. What is hard for one can be effortless for another, not because doing the thing itself is easy or hard, but because the person who is doing it made it so as a result of the station he has tuned his frequency to. It is this station alone that produced the path of least resistance and made what is hard for another effortless for him. Certainly, there are tasks in this world that can be considered and perceived as "hard work" or "hard tasks," but even these hard tasks end up being effortless for those who desire, believe, and commit to them.

Why is it that there are so many in this world who work "much harder" than the people they work for and end up making less than 1% of what the people they work for make? How could anyone even allow something like this to happen? If it weren't for all the "hard workers" doing what they do, the people they work for wouldn't even be in business!

So then, what is it? What differentiates those who are at the top of the

The Illusion of Hard Work

the chain and those who are working for them? Why is it that those who employ make far more than their employees? Well, the key differentiation between the average employer and the average employee is the direction toward where they are concentrating their attention, or, in other words, what they are "working hard" toward.

You see, employers are usually concentrating on themselves and their creations, while their employees are concentrating more on their jobs than themselves.

Look, there is nothing wrong with working for somebody else or being an employee. There are many employees who are comfortable with their jobs and even love their environment and what they do. I'm not telling you to quit your job if you enjoy doing it and are content. If you are not, however, I am offering you the possibility to do it on your own terms so you can concentrate more on yourself than somebody else.

You must know something. Throughout the duration of your period working for someone else, you will never surpass the amount of money being made by the person you're working for. Your employer will always earn more than you.

The reason employers will always earn more than their employees is because they bear the financial risk and responsibility of operating the business, and in return, reap the financial rewards of the business's success. An employee does not bear the risk that the employer bears, such as making a profit after rent, utilities, materials, and salaries.

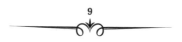

The Illusion of Hard Work

Therefore, you see, hard work is not what you think it is. Hard work is concentrated attention. The more you can concentrate your attention on a particular object or task, the harder you are working on it, and the more you desire to concentrate on that particular task, the less effort it will take for you to concentrate on it. This is why they say it is not work if you love your job.

So then, how can we dissolve the illusion of hard work so we can make money effortlessly? Well, if you have not trained your attention and willpower, then it may take some effort to train before it can become effortless. Strong Desire will aid you greatly. Once you have trained your attention and willpower, not only will hard work be effortless for you, everything you direct your trained attention and willpower to will seem this way, including making money and living a prosperous life.

Begin with building a desire and training your attention. Desire and concentrate more on improving yourself than anything else in your life. If you improve yourself, everything in your life will improve; this is simply law. Stop working harder on your job than you do on yourself. You will realize that as you begin to desire and concentrate on improving yourself more than you would on your job, your job will not only become easier, but you will be better at it.

Begin to change your beliefs about yourself and your world and tune your frequency to the station of infinite desire power and infinite willpower. Earnestly tell yourself, "I do anything I say I will. I have strong willpower. I am a hard worker. Hard work is effortless for me."

The Illusion of Hard Work

As you persistently concentrate your attention on your desire, you will begin passing the performance of the work you're doing onto the subconscious where it will manifest into effortless action. Continue to train your willpower habitually and your subconscious forces will turn it into one that does anything you command it to do.

You see, you do what you do because you are who you are, and you do what you do effortlessly because who you are does it automatically. If you conceive yourself to be someone who always makes mistakes, does things wrong, or never amounts to anything, then surely you will project these beliefs and come across experiences that reflect them.

Taking action is but the net result of being, and without being who you are, you would not be doing what you're doing. Almost everything we do, we have trained ourselves to do, and with a prolonged concentrated attention, we gradually end up doing it automatically.

When you first learn how to drive, it may be challenging at first, and you may need to utilize a lot of conscious effort in practicing again and again until you get it right. After you get it right, it gets passed onto the subconscious, where the driving begins to seem like it is being done automatically for you with little to no conscious effort.

Everything in life begins with training and ends up being automatic if we commit to concentrating on it habitually. Take walking as another example. When we were toddlers, it took us some time to learn how to walk. What about now? Do you have to think about walking?

The Illusion of Hard Work

Most human behaviors and expressions are done without thinking. 95% of one's life is controlled by their irrational and automatic subconscious mind, which we have called herein the "station" you tune your frequency to. You can now consider your station to be your subconscious program.

With that being said, you must realize that 95% of what we do requires no real willpower, as it is done automatically according to the station we're tuned to. He who you deem a hard worker in your eyes is but himself in his eyes. His hard work is done automatically according to who he has created himself to be and the station he has chosen to tune his frequency to.

How can we train our will if almost everything we do automatically requires little to no will? How can we concentrate our attention if we have nothing we really need to concentrate on? Well, since it's already effortless for us to do things we already do on a daily basis, we must begin directing our attention to concentrating on new things and asserting our willpower as we're doing it. Throughout this workbook, you will have exercises for you to train your attention and willpower, but for now, I will give you basic practices that will improve both your ability to concentrate and your willpower.

A practice you can begin now is deliberately concentrating on an everyday task. When you eat, focus and concentrate on the taste of the food, the texture of it, the smell of it, and the look of it. If your mind goes wandering and thinking about something other than the food you

The Illusion of Hard Work

are eating, gently bring your attention back to the food and concentrate on eating it until you are finished. While doing this may seem silly, you are not only training your attention, but also training your willpower by directing your attention back to the task at hand.

Soon enough, you will come to realize that you are the controller of not only everything you do, but everything you think about, everything you believe to be true, and everything you create. If you don't already know this to be true, it is because you have not trained your willpower enough to the point where you literally control everything, from your mind to your actions to your emotions, on command.

Don't be a victim of those who tell you limiting beliefs such as, "It is impossible for people like us to become rich. We're not lucky enough to make money. Only the people at the top are wealthy. To live a prosperous life, you must be born into a prosperous family. You have to get a job in order to make money. You have to work hard on everything but yourself, only then you will make money."

These are beliefs that have been instilled into society to keep us from creating a prosperous life for ourselves. Since that is the station most people are operating in, you must keep your station private, for they understand and know not of the station you have tuned your mind to, only their own. Begin now to tune your frequency to the station of determined concentration and begin to believe you are a powerful, deliberate, and incredibly hard worker. Soon, you will find that everything that was once hard is now effortless for you.

I AM

Your life is the cause of two words: I AM. I AM is your life, in truth. I AM is pure unconditioned awareness — the pure unconditioned mind. I AM is innocent and all-knowing. I AM only knows yes, and accepts as true all that you say I AM to. I AM automatically expresses all that is impressed upon it. I AM is the firsthand cause, and that which you say I AM to creates the effect that projects your reality. I AM is the one unconditioned mind infinitely conditioned to create, perceive, and experience, the one unconditioned consciousness infinitely expressing itself as the Creator.

There is no moment in time that you don't think, feel, or know I AM. I AM is your very essence. It is who you were before you created yourself to be your name, your body, your gender, your personality, your qualities, and your values, and it is still who you are beneath the surface of your identity and beyond the role of the character you chose to play in this lifetime. It is the real you behind the mask you wear, and it is the very essence of not only you, but everything in the entire Universe. I AM the Oneness and Unity of all things.

All things that proceed I AM is what you create I AM to be. This creates who and what you're aware of being. It conditions the unconditioned consciousness and creates the lens through which you view yourself and your world. Essentially, I AM is the radio that contains within itself an infinite number of stations and an infinite number of potential frequencies that we can tune our mind to receive information from.

To attract prosperity, you must first claim it in consciousness. It must

I AM

be engrained into your being by becoming a part of your I AM. In this world, you only attract what you are in being. If your beliefs about yourself and your world do not include being prosperous or having the capabilities to create avenues and streams of income, then you will be seeking a life that does not exist within your being, and thus cannot exist within your outer world.

These are what affirmations are for. Affirmations are what create your I AM. As you proceed with the workbook section of this book, you will find numerous mantras and affirmations that a prosperous and wealthy state of consciousness contains, which you can also use to assert and claim the same state as true of yourself and your world.

Essentially, the affirmations we provide for you, if earnestly accepted as true, are what will tune your frequency to the station of prosperity. Soon enough, you will find that your mind will no longer contain thoughts of lack and limitation, thoughts of unworthiness and fear; they will be replaced with thoughts of abundance and power, and thoughts of confidence and faith.

During the period when you are reading and writing affirmations, you must not just read and write them; you must claim them by feeling and knowing them to be true of yourself and your world. You must tap into the feeling of naturalness, satisfaction, and fulfillment that comes as a result of accepting and ingraining these affirmations into your being.

Although you may think that you only speak things into existence

I AM

when using words, you also manifest things into existence by feeling yourself to be that which was once spoken but no longer needs to be said. Something that you already know to be true about yourself and your world but no longer need to use words to express it, such as confidence, for example. A confident being does not need to affirm his confidence with words. He affirms it by being it and expresses it automatically without the need to use words.

In the same way, the rich man is aware of being rich, and the poor man is aware of being poor. It is the feeling that creates the fact of what you're saying, and it is the fact that conditions your consciousness to express the way of being. As your beliefs of yourself and your world change, so will your expressions, and as your expressions change, so will your reality, for it is but the reflection of your beliefs.

There is only one time when the words I AM may be referred to, and that time is the everlasting now. When you use the words I AM, you are not referring to something in the future or the past; I AM refers to the awareness of being here and now. I AM contains all that was and will ever be in the infinite present moment. If you would like to successfully alter your state of consciousness, when you write your affirmations in the present tense, write and feel I AM rather than "I will" and "I have" rather than "I want." The terms "I will" and "I want" do not exist here and now. "I will" may exist or may not exist in the future, for one that continuously says, "I will," also says that they are not here and now. The will to be exists now, for all is expressed now. I AM is effortless. I AM is being here and now.

I AM

Similarly, when you say, "I want this," the signal you're sending is that you don't have it here and now. When you say, "I will be that person one day," the signal you're sending is that you are not that person here and now. In circumstances like this, you are not affirming what you're saying; you're affirming the feeling of not being or having what you say here and now.

Again, you attract what you are, not what you will be. You attract more of what you have, not what you want. Therefore, I tell you, feel it to be true and rest in the satisfaction of it being so. Feel prosperous and abundant affirmations to be true of yourself and your world and express yourself as that person. Walk like that person would, talk like that person would, and act as that person would. Most importantly, think like that person would think, and feel like that person would feel.

Stop looking outside of yourself and look within to find the real cause of your current position. Don't let your current position create you. Create your current position. We are either creating our life or being created by it, and if we are being created by it, then we have no power within ourselves, for we forget about the only power that creates it all.

Look within, and you will find the I AM within you. You will find it is the same I AM as everybody else beneath the surface of their mask. You will find that I AM is the only truth and the only cause that will ever be able to release what you have created it to be. You are not the I AM you created. You are, I AM. To be someone you're currently not, you must die in the I AM you created and be reborn into the I AM you desire.

Your Current Position

Look around you. Do you like your current position? Your job? Your home? Your surroundings? Your life? If you do, then you're in luck. You can use the evidence of your physical reality to work in your favor to reaffirm that you're already living the life you desire. If you don't like your current position, you must take your attention away from the evidence of your physical reality and put it on the evidence of your imagination. Why do that? Because imagination creates reality, and everything you're experiencing is the cause of your imaginal activity.

Your current state of consciousness is the cause of your current position. What you currently see in your physical reality is the physical manifestation of the state you dwell in. Your life can't change unless you change your state of consciousness, and you can't do that until you begin to think feelingly of ideas that are in harmony with the life you desire. This is why one must never look at their outside world if they wish to change it, for it is like looking in a mirror and expecting its reflection to change. When one realizes that there is nothing to change but self in this life, one becomes the master of self and life.

You see, we live in a world of objectified states. In order to attract a new life, we must be mentally occupied in that state. To do this, rather than concentrating on a physical reality you do not desire, direct your attention to concentrating on visualizing the life you desire to live. Begin thinking of new ideas that are in harmony with your vision, and change your beliefs accordingly. Do this, and you will be reborn. Revalue and expand everything you believe to be true about yourself, and you will be rewarded with new thoughts and a new life.

Your Current Position

Deny your current position and command the life you desire to live. Feel as you would feel if it were true, and think from this vision you have created. This feeling will project a series of events that will inevitably lead you to the realization of your vision. As you allow your new state of consciousness to be naturally expressed through you, this series of events will take you from your current position to the position you've embodied in your imagination. You may not be able to see it happen, for it is only once you reach your destination that you can connect the dots backward; however, you will certainly be able to feel it happening right before you.

What stops many from progressing is an undesirable position. We let our current position or circumstances guide us and we forget to guide ourselves. Rather than creating our current position, we are stuck in the cycle of our current position creating us.

If your current position is keeping you in an undesirable state, take your attention away from it and go to your true guide, the guide that created your state and current position — your wonderful imagination. If you look for answers in the state of consciousness and position you don't want to be in, all you will find are the answers conforming to what you don't want, such as, "I can't make this much money because of my current circumstance," or, "My current position doesn't allow me to do what I want to do." In this limiting state of consciousness, you remain in an endless loophole, stuck looking to change your current position by looking at your current position. One can never change the outside world without first changing the inside world.

Your Current Position

Rely on the evidence of your imagination, and you will recondition your awareness from "I can't make this much money because of my current circumstance" to "I can make this much money regardless of my circumstance because I know who I am; I know my destination, and I can see it clearly in my mind's eye." You see, moments ago, you were merely aware of being stuck in your current position with no way out, but now, as you vividly imagine and create a new state, you're suddenly aware of being free from your current position.

Earnestly repeat and feel an affirmation such as, "I can, regardless of my current position, and I AM, regardless of what life tells me," if you wish to ascend beyond the limitations created by the created self. With a new state of consciousness comes a new state of being. Rather than facing hardships, you will face opportunities to un-become what you were programmed to become, and rather than facing obstacles, you will face opportunities to become who you desire to be.

Our subconscious mind is incapable of distinguishing between imagination and reality. There is no separation, according to the subconscious mind. By simply feeling what you imagine as true, you will ultimately impress your subconscious and express it in your outer world. Seeing it in your imagination and feeling it is true will create the fact. It is only through the medium of feeling that we can communicate with I AM. Emotion is energy in motion, and when you think a thought, you are transforming the Universe's static (stationary) energy into dynamic (moving) energy. When you feel the thought, that dynamic energy is projected into your outer world.

Your Current Position

Not our thoughts, but our mental attitude from them is what gets expressed. When you imagine a reality of abundance and success, your attitude will go from not having any money due to your current position to feeling as though you are already wealthy, regardless of your current position. Neville Goddard said it best when he said: "Everything depends upon our attitude towards ourselves. That which we will not affirm as true of ourselves cannot develop in our life."

Our mental attitude is the only means through which we can accept new thoughts, new possibilities, and a new life. Everything we desire is solely waiting for our acceptance. Many rely on their outer world to control their mental attitude, but this is a major mistake. When you let the outer world control how you think and feel, the world takes all of your power, and you remain powerless. You become a victim of the world rather than the creator of it. You accept as true only what the world tells you and deny the possibility of what is not in the world.

Just as you can become a victim of the world, you can become a victim of your past. Think of your past. What meaning do you give it? Through what attitude do you give it meaning? What is the story you created from it? Did it make you strong or weak? What do you accept as a result of your past? Are you willing to change your story and rewrite it?

Just as your imagination can free you from the past, it can keep you locked up in it. Through the power of feeling your imaginal activity, the past, present, and future exist simultaneously in the everlasting eternal now. Let go of the past and the world, and be the creator again.

Resentment

If you believe money is only for a certain group of people (a group that does not include yourself), you will unconsciously resent money and the people with it. A mental attitude like this will push you further and further away from living a prosperous life. Consider life a reflection of all that we feel to be true.

If we accept the wrong ideas about money and the people with it — or anything we desire, for that matter — life will consider these beliefs as things we don't want rather than things we truly desire. Everything we attract is harmoniously done by law. In order to attract a wealthy, abundant, and prosperous life, we must never feel resentment toward it or condemn those who have money. We must build a strong relationship between the abundance of money available beyond the illusions of limitation and the many people who obtain it.

Resentment is usually a companion emotion to envy and jealousy. "Why do they have it, and I don't?" or, "She doesn't deserve what she has. I should be the one with it." If you want to live an abundant and prosperous life, you must look at others living that life in gratitude, as you would be for yourself if you were in the same position. In truth, what makes us feel this way is our own burning desire to be in the position they are in. Rather than feeling jealous or resentful, cheer them on so they can become more wealthy, abundant, and prosperous. Be proud of them for the powerful frequency they emit. Acknowledge and appreciate their success consciousness rather than resenting them for having what you truly want.

Resentment

If you are in this position, consciously or unconsciously, change your assumptions about money. Consider money not as something hard to achieve, and most certainly not something reserved only for those chosen to possess and make it. You must see money as something easily attainable for yourself. Beliefs like "Money is difficult to get" or that it takes hard work will hold you back. As we discussed, difficulty and hard work are illusions created by your current state of consciousness. When you can accept and fully believe you are the person you desire to be, everything else happens automatically. All difficulty and hard work become effortless automatic expressions.

Resentment for money stems from misconceptions about money. So many cannot live a plentiful life because they think it is reserved only for those born into it, those who got "lucky," or those with special connections. Many who harbor resentment toward money also seem not to have such a strong relationship with those who possess it. They walk around town, seeing people with luxury cars and condemning them for having such luxurious goods that they truly desire to have themselves. They watch a video of someone living a life they dream of living, and they subconsciously say, "Wow! What a show-off," or, "You don't actually own any of that," or, "Must be nice to be born into generational wealth." People may consider a life of abundance to be the cause of luck, race, gender, location, or circumstances. Know that none of these play any role in obtaining a wealthy life. The only cause of a wealthy life is a wealthy state of consciousness that expresses itself as such.

Resentment

Let's take Jaime Parker as an example. Jamie Parker, a top-tier and top-producing banker, is in the midst of a meeting with some extremely successful clients and investors. Jamie had recently welcomed her colleague to her team and invited him to this meeting so she could show him the ropes. Jamie's natural state of consciousness is critical to acknowledge. Her natural state is one of abundance, courage, confidence, specified knowledge, and success. Jamie has been in this profession for some time and, as a result, has accumulated a generous amount of money and is now living a plentiful life. She closes the most contracts, attracts the best clientele, and earns the most money out of all other bankers in the company.

On the other hand, her coworker is currently in a state of unworthiness, lack, fear, and doubt. He tries to justify why he is unable to close any contracts through limiting beliefs such as, "I'm just not receiving any good leads," or, "There are only a select few people who can truly succeed in the company, and I know I'm not one of them." He doesn't know that it is due to comments like these that he attracts his results, position, and role in the company. He makes every effort to place blame on someone or something outside of his own state.

During the meeting, Jamie introduced her colleague to the rest of her team. Everything was going well as he introduced himself to everyone. Once Jamie's team began speaking about their massive success, her colleague felt uncomfortable. It seemed as though Jamie and the success of her team began to annoy and frustrate her colleague. He

Resentment

unknowingly began to build a resentful perspective toward Jamie and her team solely due to their different beliefs. Jamie's colleague had limiting beliefs that prevented him from accepting possibilities that were not in harmony with his current ones. The frequency he tuned his station to prevented him from accepting what he did not feel was true of himself and his world.

Jamie's colleague dwelled in a different state of consciousness. He had tuned his frequency to a station of lack and limitation. Jamie's colleague felt uncomfortable due to his new vibrational environment and did everything he could to protect the station he was tuned to, the self he created. He felt threatened because he was not used to being in a room filled with successful, confident, and wealthy people. Jamie's colleague unconsciously condemned everyone on the team because he could only attract what he believed to be true of himself. His jealousy was projected by his own burning desire to be like them. The jealousy reflected back to him as he unknowingly continued to attract the circumstances he faced due to his programmed conditions. Even though he may truly want to be a part of Jamie's team, he could not express himself as someone who belonged in the team.

Given that everything is harmoniously attracted by law, it's understandable why Jamie's colleague felt uneasy during the meeting. Her colleague could only attract others who operate at the same frequency; similarly, Jamie and her team could have only attracted others who operate at the same frequency.

Resentment

This is not to say that Jamie's colleague had no chance; however, the opportunity was entirely up to him. Option one was for him to continue to unconsciously resent Jaime and her team while living his life in the ways of his limiting state, and option two was for him to choose to appreciate Jamie's team and the beliefs they held. Rather than resenting them with jealousy, he would be inspired by them. Rather than seeing their success as something that threatened him, he would learn from it and apply it to his everyday life.

If he chose the first option, he would have remained where he was, and if he chose option two, he would have seen Jamie and her team through a different lens, a lens of inspiration and possibility. He chose the second option, and his life was never the same. He began to see the potential and possibilities, slowly accepting as true of himself what Jamie and her team believed to be true about themselves. He rose in consciousness and tuned his frequency to the same station as Jaime and her team. His new beliefs harmonized with his surroundings as he finally began to attract success and wealth into his life.

You see, then, you cannot despise, condemn, and resent those who have what you want. Our attitude tunes our station just as our thoughts do, and we can only attract the station we are tuned to. Everything is attracted to us by law. The people, places, things, and circumstances we need to get from point A to point B are attracted by law. Let go of resentment and begin to appreciate and admire those who manifest the same desires as you, if you ever dare to do the same.

Mastermind

Everyone's mind is tuned to a specific station of the Universe. A mastermind is established and created when multiple minds are tuned to the same station. It occurs when the minds of individuals come together with the same vision, inspiration, and desire. Each and every individual taps into a different state of consciousness to fulfill the roles required to realize the entirety of a vision. Once one mind turns into a collective mind, the ability to realize a vision becomes inevitable. The bigger the collective, the bigger the vision becomes.

One mind can realize the entirety of a vision by tuning itself to the possibilities required to realize it, but one mind cannot be tuned to two stations simultaneously. Just as you can only do one thing at a time, your mind can only concentrate on one thing at a time. Although we can multitask through our subconscious forces, like driving a car and talking on the phone simultaneously or typing on a keyboard while at the same time looking at the computer screen, it takes multiple minds to operate, automate, and realize a vision or ideal, especially if there are multiple skills, behaviors, and specialized knowledge required to realize the vision. Each role in a company or venture represents its own frequency. The more complex and greater a vision, the more minds are required for the vision to be realized. If you were to speed up the process of realizing your vision, you must create a collective mastermind.

A restaurant, for example, has many roles, varying on the food they serve and the offers they provide. One mind can be trained and tuned

Mastermind

to the frequency of answering phone calls and helping customers, while another mind can be tuned to the frequency of cooking meals, another tuned to placing orders, and another tuned to overseeing everything.

All companies run this way. This is not to say that one mind can't do all that was stated. It starts with the one mind, your mind, tuning itself to the possibilities required for the vision to be realized, and then training others to tune their frequency to the appropriate stations. However, if you proceed solely by yourself, it will result in a company that will be limited to one mind when it can be extended to serve even more people. If you wish to provide a satisfactory product or service, you must provide your customers or clients with a great experience. If you wish to grow or scale your company, you must find others who are already tuned to the frequency required, or you must train them to tune their frequency to the required station.

Although training is inevitable if you were to realize your vision, you can find minds who are already trained and experienced and can guide you to realizing your vision. Building a mastermind doesn't only involve creating and realizing different roles; a mastermind helps find solutions to problems, attracts new ideas, and improves the overall flow of the operation. A successful mastermind must not only serve the roles of the vision, but also love the vision and be inspired by it.

If part of the collective does not have faith or believe in the vision, the

Mastermind

vision may just be rendered lifeless. A collective mind operates best when inspired (in spirit), and inspiration comes with a purpose or a passion. You can provide all the individuals in your mastermind with opportunities to express themselves fully by showing them that your vision creates a difference in the world. If your vision aligns with serving others by making a difference or a transformation, it will inspire others, and as a result, others will be compelled to realize it. It would be wise to ensure each individual of the mastermind plays the role they truly desire. This will also ensure that your vision contains the love required for it to be realized to its maximum potential.

Building a mastermind is not always easy. The creator must train other minds. In most cases, many roles, maybe even roles you may not have known of before, must be created and mastered for a business to operate to its fullest. If the purpose of your vision is not to serve others, you will be serving the self, which is an illusion. The path to serving yourself will merely leave you chasing temporary pleasures. It will ultimately leave you unsatisfied without knowing the real reason why. It is only by serving others that one can truly ever be satisfied in this world, for it is the very purpose of being here on earth.

When one serves the illusion of the self, one sees no wrongs in what they do. They could sell drugs, open bars, and create products and services that not only harm individuals but also themselves. This will eventually result in guilt, shame, and a loss of purpose. Only those who know their intentions are good can be prosperous and fulfilled.

Being

If you were to ever free yourself from the being you have created, you must first seek beyond it and find the Being that has never been and will never be created. The Being within you that is beyond the being you created. The Being that is changeless, formless, infinite, and all-knowing. The Being that contains within itself an infinite amount of possibilities waiting to be expressed through your acceptance of them.

In order to tune our frequency to the station of abundance and prosperity, we must see beyond the station we are currently tuned to. We cannot merely turn off the station of our mind; as much as we may try to, the station will continue replaying itself over and over until it is re-tuned to a new frequency. You can identify your station by being consciously aware of the thoughts and imaginal activities that arise from the station.

Sit down in a comfortable position, close your eyes, and concentrate on your breath. Still your mind to the best of your ability by making your primary focus your breath. If thoughts arise, gently bring your attention back to your breath. Ensure you are fully relaxed and your mind is still. This very stillness and silence is the nature of your being. Notice how pleasant and peaceful it is. Notice how much love you feel from simply being here, now, with no worries, no thoughts, and nothing to do. Notice how you have transcended beyond the station of your *conditioned thinking mind* and entered the station of the *unconditioned knowing mind*, the station of infinite possibility, the station of the Universal Mind. Here, you observe what you created.

Being

The mind creates it all. From the building you dwell in to the bed you sleep in. From the car you drive to the roads you drive on. All things physical must come from the non-physical; all matter must come from Spirit. Spirit is found within your unconditioned mind. You do not need to believe what I am telling you. I am speaking from experience, and only from your own experience can you open your eyes to seeing the truth that will set you free. Experience it now. Imagine a rose and smell it. Imagine a basketball and feel it. Through your unconditioned mind, you do not need to wait to experience what you desire. Your experiences are merely waiting to be found within your imagination.

Experience does not exist outside of you. It exists within you. All experiences outside of you are merely the experiences you choose to create within your imagination. Therefore, all of your outer world experiences are contingent upon what you experience within your imagination. If you desire change in your outer world, you must create the change first in your inner world by tapping into your unconditioned mind and seeing beyond the world you created.

Your life reflects everything you accept as true about yourself and the world. Life will ultimately reward you for who you're aware of being and what you're aware of having. Ask yourself, "Who and what am I aware of being?" Am I aware of being rich, middle class, or poor? Am I aware of being courageous or cowardly? Whichever you accept as true will create the experience you are accepting, and the experience you accept will merely echo the station you have tuned your frequency to.

Being

What you do naturally is the effect of the station you are tuned to. The station you are tuned to contains all you accept and feel to be true about yourself and your world. You wake up and do what you do because you are who you are. You brush your teeth, take a shower, and make breakfast. You don't have to think or try to do any of these; they are effortless and automatic because of the station you have tuned your mind to.

Let us take John as an example. John is an entrepreneur with multiple eight- to nine-figure businesses. His frequency is tuned to confidence, success, wealth, and knowledge. This station is expressed automatically by running his businesses, accessing meetings, etc. For John, this is another day in his life. He does not have to think about any of it. As a result of John being who he is, he attracts multi-million-dollar ideas and effortlessly executes and materializes them. It is as if, no matter what, opportunities continuously present themselves in outer world experiences solely for him to continue living the life he has accepted as true.

John has people approaching him asking, "How are you motivated to do all of this? How are you able to work this hard? Don't you ever get tired of working?" John's reply follows, "It isn't hard, and I don't get tired of it because this is just who I AM. It is a lifestyle for me. It is a way of being."

People think that there is something special about John, but in reality,

Being

John is the same as you and me. The only difference is that John experiences reality through the nature of the being he has created. John sees himself as the person he desires to be within his imagination, so he effortlessly does what he does because his station automatically expresses it, and his life automatically reflects it. Life gives him multimillion-dollar ideas because the station he tuned his frequency to is the station that receives them naturally.

It is only when you look beyond the being you created and enter the Being you are that you can create and manifest the being of your liking by visualizing, feeling, and believing you already are the being you desire to be. Rise in consciousness and enter your unconditioned mind so you can disregard the reasoning of the limited being preventing you from creating the being you desire. Commit to being your highest self by committing to doing the right thing always. Continue on the path of righteousness, and your new frequency will provide you with the same multimillion-dollar ideas, and you will know that no matter what the outer world shows you, you are wealthy regardless.

Just as poverty is a state of consciousness, wealth, prosperity, and abundance are nothing more than states of consciousness. The key difference between these states is that one is your birthright, while the other is a mental disease. Choose wisely the state you wish to embody, for again, you cannot be in two states simultaneously. Your life will ultimately reward you for the station you tune your frequency, for your station is that which you will express automatically.

Desire

Desire is our nature. It is the only force of power that exists within the entire Universe. One may merely want something or think wishfully of what he wants, but the one who wants something more than anything else will inevitably receive the fruits of his desire. You see, we are all born with desires, but each of these desires varies in degree. You could merely desire something, but it won't affect you too much if you don't get it. This is what we call a wishful thought, a life-less want. Having wishful thoughts will take you nowhere in life, for they have no life to give. Only when one cultivates a burning desire for something they want more than anything can they be willing to sacrifice anything for it. It is here, through this burning desire, that you create your calling, your passion, your purpose, and your destiny.

Many do not know how to truly want or desire in this world. It is often not until one is faced with the extreme difficulty of life slapping them in the face that one cultivates the desire to change their life. This is often what it takes for one to be transformed, but I tell you that it doesn't have to be this way. You can be transformed only if you want it enough, and you cannot want it enough if you see no reason to be transformed, for you will not be hungry to be transformed.

The burning desire I speak of is the same desire of the man who is starving and desires to eat, a woman stranded in the desert with no water who desires to drink, and a mother or a father with their child in danger who desires to save their child. When one taps into this degree of desire, he also taps into the cosmic and infinite will beyond himself.

Desire

Many believe they only have one purpose in this world, but this is false. Every strong desire you come across serves a different purpose in this world. When a desire is realized, it will manifest in its own destiny. Just as you have multiple desires, you will have multiple purposes, multiple callings, and multiple destinies. Each and every burning desire manifests a different destiny.

If you remember growing up, you were always inspired (in spirit) by your heart's desires. When someone asked you as a kid, "What do you want to be when you grow up?" you experienced feelings of desire, love, and purpose with no limitation. You answered confidently and without a doubt, "I want to be an astronaut!" Fast forward to today; the confidence may not be the same, as your ability to desire has changed and diminished due to the identity you created by your beliefs about yourself and your world.

When you were a kid, you didn't see any limitations that would stop you from being the person you desired to be. Before developing your conscious mind, you didn't think such limitations existed. You were still a new soul, fully in spirit, believing anything was possible through your imagination. You could desire anything you want without a doubt in sight. You came from a place of pure imagination, pure love, bliss, infinite power, and infinite intelligence, where all potentials and possibilities exist, and you had everything you could possibly want if you were to just want it enough. We are now afraid to desire big things solely due to the doubts of our conditioned minds.

Desire

Our goal is to return to the same state as we once were. A state where we can use our imagination to create our reality, where we don't need to think about the doubts and limitations preventing us from tapping into this part of our imagination, so we can begin to truly desire without fear, and know it is possible because there truly is no such thing as failure. We want to return to the state where we failed hundreds of times before we could finally succeed and still know deep down that success was inevitable, such as learning to walk.

Again, you were born to desire. Our true power is desire power, from our first steps to our last words. You were born to let love guide you. Desire as you once did without limitation. Choose now to go back to when you didn't worry about when or how something will happen and merely assumed it was done. Realize that without desire, there wouldn't be a desire to move, breathe, or feel. A desireless being is a life-less being.

Let love retake its course. Identify the petty, deluded desires preventing you from realizing what you truly and so greatly desire. Cultivate a burning desire and sacrifice those no longer serving you. You must pay the price if you were to realize your full potential. You must sacrifice the temporary desires stopping you from actualizing your permanent desires. Transform fear of desiring to change because you believe something bad will happen to the faith of knowing that your burning desire to change will cause you to tap into your cosmic will and create a ripple effect of miracles for all who cross your path.

Realizing Your Vision to Completion

Manifestations of wealth result from thoughts, visions, or ideas that generate wealth. Wealth is not something that falls from the sky, it is the effect of realizing a vision that generates it, the expression of a station that is tuned to the frequency of serving others.

The essence of manifesting is consciously creating your reality, and you do this first by having a goal, aim, or desire and then realizing it. We will refer to the goals, aims, and desires herein as visions. Realizing your vision to completion can be viewed and understood as planning and finalizing the necessary steps that it will take for your vision to be manifested. You must first plan before you act. If you act without a plan, you will be aimless in your expression.

Contradicting as it may seem, we tell you to "not worry about when or how your vision will manifest" while simultaneously telling you that you must realize and plan your vision accordingly for it to be manifested. The key is realizing it not through worry but trust, for it is only through trust that you can realize your vision in the first place.

Two can ask, "How am I going to manifest it?" One can ask the question through worry, while the other can ask the question through trust and confidence. The one asking through worry has his door closed to possibilities as he tries to plan his vision by working with his outer world, expressing uncertainty while simultaneously trying to figure out what he needs to do, without realizing that it is the very attitude that comes from "needing" to do something that is causing worry.

Realizing Your Vision to Completion

On the other hand, the one who is asking the question with trust and confidence has his door open to the possibilities of how his vision can be realized. He realizes he doesn't "need" to do anything, for everything is already done since he knows his destination. He disregards his outer world if it is not in alignment with his vision and begins thinking *from* the vision rather than just merely thinking *of* the vision.

Despite not currently knowing the plan or the initial steps to take for you to realize your vision, you must live as if it's already done if you wish to create the means through which the plan and initial steps can drop into your awareness. Disregard your reasoning mind by taking your attention away from your outer world and the "how" will present itself.

Just as we discussed in previous chapters, for us to tune our frequency into a new station, we must step out of our current station to allow the information of the new station to pass through us. We cannot realize any vision if our current attitude toward our vision contains worry, doubt, and limitation.

For example, if I were to have a strong desire to open a restaurant, though the idea is currently just a thought, I would imagine it being done. I would imagine the grand opening with a large line of people waiting to try our new food. I would imagine smiles on everyone's faces as they enjoy our food. I would imagine cooking in the kitchen and making friends with our customers. I would see my bank account

Realizing Your Vision to Completion

balance increase, and feel the satisfaction and gratitude of having the restaurant up, running, and successful. If thoughts of worry or doubt were to arise, I would simply not identify with them. I would take my attention away from them and put it toward feeling possibilities of the opposite nature as true. I would earnestly assert affirmations that are in alignment with the restaurant up and running.

If I continued living my life in the assumption that what I imagined was true, all of the thoughts and ideas to realize the vision would begin presenting themselves, and my vision would begin to realize itself. I would claim and accept it is done. I would release the worry of when and how it will happen by trusting in divine timing and order, knowing that I would face a sequence of events that would provide me with everything I need not only to realize my vision, but manifest it.

At this moment, I would begin learning what I needed to learn, thinking what I needed to think, and doing what I needed to do, without "needing" to do it. Thoughts to realize the vision would present themselves, and my burning desire would be expressed according to the cosmic will that would compel me to take the necessary actions to realize it. My burning desire would drive me to study and see how other restaurants run their business. The station I tuned my frequency to would give me all the answers to my questions. If I did not have the money to open the restaurant in the first place, I would disregard it. How will I get the money? Trust and knowing. I would assume that I already had the funds for my business to be open and thriving.

Think from Your Vision

If one desires to manifest a prosperous and wealthy life, he must visualize himself living at the end of his journey and think from that vision as though he is already living that life. It is one thing to think of a wealthy life and another to think from the state of already living a wealthy life. When one merely thinks of living a wealthy life one day, he is desirelessly wishful thinking of a time that does not exist. However, when one thinks from the state of already living a wealthy life, he makes the future a present fact, and, as a result, he tunes his frequency to the station of wealth and is presented with every possibility to manifest that reality.

Regardless of whether or not you have a plan, go into your imagination and see yourself already living an abundant, wealthy, and prosperous life. See the vividness of being in your dream home and being able to buy whatever you'd like. Feel the feelings of getting congratulated by your loved ones for the abundance you have accumulated and the generosity you have embodied and expressed by giving money to those you love and those in need. Imagine driving your dream car, looking at your abundant bank account, and experiencing all you would experience in your outer world. Feel all that is contained in your destination, and make your destination a present fact, here and now.

Continue living from that vision. Walk like that person, talk like that person, think like that person, do like that person, be like that person. Regardless of whether or not your physical reality tells you it is true, carry on knowing that vision is your reality.

Think from Your Vision

Continue training your imagination through visualization until it gets so vivid and real that you experience a sensation of desire power that will cause you to shed tears. You begin to cry out of out of love, power, and gratitude for all that is and all that will be. You know in your heart that it is done. You feel the business is already opened and thriving. You feel the money being accumulated. You feel the feelings that would be yours were you living the life of your dreams, and you make that life a present reality.

Do not just visualize once in a blue moon and think you are done. You cannot imagine a wealthy life one day and a life of lack the next. If you desire to live this life, you must commit to accepting it forever. You must sacrifice your current reality for the reality you truly desire. You must pay the price of your current state if you wish to express the state you desire. I tell you again, you cannot be in two states simultaneously. You are either in one or another.

Do not say that you will be that person one day. When you say you will be that person one day, you are sacrificing day one of being that person. There is no tomorrow. There is only here and now. Call out to the essence of your very being and earnestly say, "I AM! I CAN! I WILL! I KNOW!" There is no I will be in the future. Your will is not something that can be put into action at a later time. Your willpower can only be used and unlocked now through I AM. Begin now to think FROM your vision rather than just merely thinking of your vision. It is only up to you to make your future dream a present reality.

Think from Your Vision

Are you willing to take your attention away from your senses and trust in your imagination? Are you able to trust in yourself regardless of who the world created you to be? Begin now, therefore, and call upon your will to do as you would were you to be living the reality of wealth you so deeply desire. Train your willpower now if you ever wish to have it at your disposal with ease. Be the one from your vision, and there will be no choice but for that vision to be realized.

Stop worrying about the when and the how. Surrender in trust and have real confidence take over. Opportunities will present themselves, and everything you could possibly need will be provided in divine timing and divine order. Earnestly assert your abundant and wealthy nature. Feel it and trust it until it becomes your natural state. Feel it until you have no doubts in your mind and no fear in your heart.

Do not tell anyone of your claims or visions. Let them observe, and you will see that they will also reflect your change. People around you will tell you it is not going to happen. Even the ones you love and trust the most will tell you it won't happen. You will have others express their limited reasoning and project their doubts and fears. Disregard it all. Don't let anything or anyone get in between you and your creation, including yourself.

What you see in your mind's eye should be kept sacred. Tell no one your vision until you have cultivated the confidence to attract it. Have others confirm the change for you. Begin now. Begin living in the end.

Mutual Exchange

Dr. Joseph Murphy once wrote, "There is no such thing as something for nothing." This means exactly what it means. You cannot receive something from the world if you give nothing to it. The only way to receive is if you first give.

Earl Nightingale said, "Prosperity is founded upon a law of mutual exchange. Any person who contributes to prosperity must prosper, in turn, himself. Sometimes, the return will not come from those you serve, but it must come to you from someplace, for that is the law."

A prosperous and abundant life can only be realized and manifested if one contributes to it by serving others with products or services that are mutually beneficial in terms of the value of the offer provided and the compensation received for the offer provided.

Money is not something that will fall from the sky, and it is surely not something manifested by those who are desireless, aimless, and do nothing to make it. Money is the effect of a cause that is a product or service. There can be no effect without a cause. You don't need to invent a life-changing product or provide others with a service that will change the entire world. However, this isn't necessarily something out of reach to anyone, unless you believe it is, of course.

A product could be as simple as a handmade bracelet or necklace that you enjoy creating for yourself and loved ones, a new card game that you created, or even this very book that you're reading. A service on the

Mutual Exchange

other hand could be as simple as giving massages, detailing cars, or cleaning homes. Maybe you're an artist or an athlete, a singer or a dancer. In this case, you may ask yourself, "What will I be offering for the money I will make?" Well, don't just think of products and services as the only way to offer solutions to a problem. Solutions to problems can also be offered through inspiration, love, passion, desire, entertainment, freedom, and more.

Maybe you're a creator and love creating videos. The smile you put on someone's face could serve them in ways that may change their mood for the entire day, week, month, or even a lifetime. Something you say may open their eyes to a new perspective or viewpoint and change everything for them. Although this may not be considered a direct product or service, it sure is a solution to a problem, and it sure is serving others.

Many of us have been stuck in a cycle of believing that it is not possible to serve others or make money doing things that we enjoy and love to do. In truth, it is possible to make money doing anything as long as your offer contains a mutual benefit for the money you will be receiving and the offer you will be providing.

We do not get paid for our time; we get paid for our value. Even if we offer our time, and get paid hourly for it, we are still only getting paid for the value we offer within that time frame. As you know, there can be someone working far more hours than someone else, and they can end

Mutual Exchange

up getting paid less than the other who worked far fewer hours. There are also instances where two work the same job for the same amount of hours, but because they work in different companies, both get paid differently. The reason for this is due to the standards set by the companies for the value and offer they provide, not for the time someone works at their company or what they are doing at the company. It is not about what someone is doing in the company getting paid more; it is how they are doing it that results in a larger pay.

We get paid for our offer. The more desire someone has for our offer, the more demand is created, and the more we receive. The more people we present our offer to, the more individuals we serve, and thus, the more we receive. The greater the value of our offer, the more of a difference we can make in the lives of those who receive our offer, and the more we receive as a result.

Once you begin thinking and asking how you can serve others, mutually beneficial ideas will naturally and effortlessly get attracted to you, not because you need to force yourself to think of these mutually beneficial ideas, but because you have risen in consciousness and tuned your frequency to the station of value, offer, service, and mutual exchange, and know what you must give to receive.

At this current moment in time, there are an infinite number of ways to serve others and receive an abundant and prosperous life in return. How much money you believe you can make is directly correlated to

Mutual Exchange

how much value you believe you can provide. This is mutual exchange. I tell you, there is enough money to go around, and there are enough ways to make money. All you must do is be open to believing it.

If you do not believe you can make money or have limiting beliefs preventing you from making the amount you desire, ask yourself in self-enquire, "What value can I offer? What skills do I have experience in? What am I good at doing and or teaching?" You will find these questions listed on the page titled "Capabilities" at the end of the workbook. You can do the self-enquire and go to the page now or before you begin the workbook section. Let your mind give you answers and possibilities, and write them down.

Those who believe they lack skills or experience, can't offer any value, and are not good at doing or teaching anything, are the way they are because they believe it to be true. In truth, there is not one person in this world who isn't good at anything, has no value whatsoever, and has no skills. It is the very attitude that stems from one's refusal to believe they are good at something and have values and skills that are blocking them from realizing what they're truly capable of. If you were to desire to continue in this limiting state and attitude, I suggest you close this book now and continue living your life as you wish.

Begin now to know your worth by desiring to know your worth. Begin now to cultivate a burning desire to be a skillful and valuable individual, knowing that these skills and services will create the very

Mutual Exchange

means through which you will live an abundant and prosperous life. Begin to believe you are valuable, and you do have skills, and you are good at things, and you will go from feeling worthless to knowing that your worth extends far beyond what money can buy. Awaken to the realization that you, in truth, are an infinite creator, creating yourself and your worth with every thought, every emotion, every behavior, and every desire. If you give nothing to the world, you will receive nothing from it. This is the law of mutual exchange, and it cannot be broken.

If you are cultivating and developing a skill that you enjoy, don't quit developing it because you don't believe you can offer value from it. You never know when you might need it. The more skills you have, the more valuable you become. Furthermore, you never know what life has in store for you, where you can use one of the skills you have acquired to your benefit for something else.

Seek who inspires you and identify what they do that inspires you. See what you are enthusiastic about. Look at the successful individuals that inspire you and study them. See how they behave and do what they do. Identify their beliefs about themselves and their world. Look at their expressions and sense how they feel when they do what they do best. Look at the value they are providing, the skills they have, and what they are most good at. If what they do inspires you, give doing what they do a try for yourself.

As you continue on your journey toward living a prosperous life of

Mutual Exchange

mutual exchange, you will come across many people who inspire you, and you will also come across people whom you will inspire. You will begin to think differently and suddenly gain ideas on how to use all of your valuable skills to serve others in ways that were never presented in your previous state. As your state of consciousness is revalued and expanded, your desires will also be. You will gain desires harmonious with your new beliefs, values, and skills, and you will begin to sacrifice the little desires for the greater ones, knowing intuitively which desires are meant for you to realize and which are meant for you to let go of.

When you tune your frequency to the station of wealth, you will find that many of your thoughts and ideas will be money-related or business-related. You will have many different plans and business ideas, some of which you will begin to realize, and others you won't, varying on the degree of power coming from your desire and potential seen in the plan or vision. If you come across an idea and plan, and you cultivate a burning desire for it, you must commit to it. The idea or plan that you desire the most is what is needed for your evolution in the scale of wealth and prosperity, as well as for the realization of your ultimate visions and destinies. If the plan fails, know you were meant to face temporary defeat, and you will come across other plans that you can use the developed skillsets you've obtained in your "failed plan."

Any amount of money can be acquired by the ones who believe it is possible. In every single success story, you will realize how the ones who did experience breakthroughs are also the ones who have failed

Mutual Exchange

countless times, but still believed. Those who have failed knew that failure was not their destination, for they knew who they were and knew where they were going. They knew that everything life was throwing at them was meant for them. They had a burning desire and were committed to serving others and earning what they do today.

The people who succeed on the path to wealth and prosperity are those with impeccable skills, which they have learned from their different plans, many of which plans have initially failed. These people have devised more plans throughout their journey than you could ever guess. They do not perceive failures as anything bad; they look at failures as opportunities to grow. They look at hardships and obstacles as miracles in disguise, knowing that they will overcome them, learn from them, and use the knowledge from their failed plans or hardships to contribute to their new plan. They commit to cultivating more skills and becoming more valuable every step toward the path to prosperity.

Most successful businessmen and businesswomen are grateful for all of their failures. If it weren't for their failures, they wouldn't have developed the knowledge and skillsets that they have today, and they surely wouldn't be in the positions they are in now. You may not realize it, but everything you have ever been through, everything you are currently going through, and everything you will be going through on your journey is merely the result of what your state of consciousness projected as the sequence of events that ensures your outer world conforms to your inner world.

Mutual Exchange

Your bridge of incidents will constantly decree failures so that you learn what you need to learn in order to realize your vision to completion. You won't know that failures are actually milestones until you reach the destination and connect the dots backward. The divine bridge of incidents may cause you to fail twenty times so that you can gather the knowledge needed to hit big on the twenty-first time.

If you are not willing to face temporary defeat, then you are not willing to learn, and you are not willing to enter the path to prosperity. You must realize that mistakes and temporary failures are necessary and not bad.

Walt Disney went bankrupt during his first animation company for having "no original ideas." Despite this, Disney continued to be the iconic brand it is today. J.K. Rowling, the author of the "Harry Potter" series, faced unemployment and was rejected by multiple publishers. The series has sold hundreds of millions of copies since and spawned a highly successful franchise. Michael Jordan was cut from his high school basketball team. He used his rejection to learn from his failures and fuel his massive success, as he continued and became one of the greatest basketball players the world has ever known. Thomas Edison, Abraham Lincoln, Oprah Winfrey, Steve Jobs, and many more of the most prosperous and successful people in the world have faced similar temporary failures and would not be where they are today if they didn't face their failures and overcome them. They now know that temporary failure is part of the journey toward success and prosperity.

Mutual Exchange

Let's take one of our client's stories as an example. Paul was inspired and wanted to pursue the world of e-commerce. He was fascinated when he saw the endless opportunities and the number of people he could sell his products to. Although he didn't have much money at the time, it did not stop him from cultivating a burning desire and visualizing himself living at the end of his vision or aim, which was the destination of owning multiple seven and eight-figure businesses. Every day, Paul would wake up and think from this vision, assuming he already owned these successful businesses.

He would watch how-to videos available for free on the web, network with people who were already in e-commerce, and consistently learn what was happening inside and outside of the world of e-commerce. He found a product, opened up his first store, and ended up getting little to no sales.

He opened up his second store two months later and failed again. He continued learning and put what he was learning into action and experience. He opened his third, fourth, and fifth stores, which all failed. After one year of constant failures, he got frustrated and began to forget the power that caused him to begin his journey in the first place. He was frustrated because he knew the ins and outs of what it took to build a successful e-commerce store and all that involved scaling the company to make seven figures or more. He knew how to market, develop the business, make the website, and brand it properly. He knew everything he needed to know, but still didn't succeed.

Mutual Exchange

He asked why this was happening to him. He showed me how hard he was trying to create a successful business, but nothing was working. He was dreading everything he was going through, feeling both defeated and disappointed, thinking he was never going to succeed as he initially imagined.

I asked him, how did you feel when you first began this journey? He replied, saying he was inspired and confident. He told me he did everything he was supposed to at the beginning of his journey. He had a burning desire, visualized himself living at the end of his vision, assumed it was already done, and felt the feelings that would be his were he to have already opened his successful companies.

I then asked him, "How do you feel now?" He realized that his frustration created a ripple effect of negative thoughts and feelings. His frustration was accompanied by worry and fear-based thoughts and beliefs. He lost the confidence he had in himself and his creations. He was no longer inspired, and no longer had a burning desire.

My advice to him was simple. I knew that, at first, he didn't take my advice seriously. My advice was for him to stop trying so hard. I told him to assume he already has multiple successful stores open and act like he was working on new stores while his other stores were automized. I told him to take his attention away from his current position and keep living his life from his vision. I encouraged him to reflect and continue as he did when he began this journey.

Mutual Exchange

He continued on his journey, but this time, rather than being frustrated, he proceeded with confidence. Instead of forcing something new, he reflected on his past trials and errors. He began learning from his mistakes and temporary failures and started to see what he could change in his next company with his new level of consciousness.

Something he realized early in his reflection was that none of his products genuinely provided enough value for his customers. His offers weren't demanding, and there weren't enough people who would think his offers were worth it. He realized he was doing everything right, except keeping the law of mutual exchange in mind when creating his companies and brands.

One night, he came across a video on social media about a brand-new product that was doing extremely well. The product was a cool-looking custom bag with many features that one could use to organize and store makeup. He read the reviews and realized the product had many errors that needed to be fixed. For the price it was being sold at, he believed it lacked a valuable offer and mutual benefit for the customer.

So, he decided to create his own version of the bag and fix the errors with one of the manufacturers he found when creating one of his previous stores. With his new level of understanding and state of consciousness, he immediately began thinking of ways to improve the bag in a way that would serve people the most. He began reviewing the comments and complaints of people who purchased the bag he gained

Mutual Exchange

inspiration from, and found that many people who purchased this bag were specifically looking for a makeup and cosmetic bag, which is what this bag was marketed for. Since there were many faults in the bag being sold, Paul saw an opportunity to fix every possible error he saw and sell his bag in accordance with the demands of the people who purchased the competitor's bag.

With this new idea in mind, he also created a different design for the bag. All of these slight variations made a night and day difference when it came to the quality of the bag, the design of the bag, and the benefits of the bag. Paul became inspired by this new idea. He grew in spirit with his burning desire and decided to go all-in on his new company. His belief in this company was stronger than any of the other ones he opened before.

When he told his peers and family that he saw potential in his product, they mocked and laughed at him, telling him to stop trying because he had already failed too many times. He disregarded them all and continued creating in silence, realizing that his environment and surroundings contained limiting beliefs he would no longer accept.

He began marketing and finally selling his new product. In his first three months, he didn't see the results he desired, but he didn't get frustrated like he had previously. This time, he believed deeply in his product. As we encouraged him to do, he proceeded as if it was just another store being tested, acting as if he already had multiple stores.

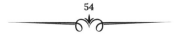

Mutual Exchange

With the expression and manifestation of the cosmic will that steamed from the fire started by his burning desire, Paul began practicing, experimenting, and learning more and more about how successful companies run. As he was studying different methodologies of marketing his bag, he realized that he was not integrating and doing much of what successful e-commerce companies would do, such as split testing paid campaigns, emails, marketing angles, and so forth.

He revised how he was marketing his bag and chose to split-test his videos and emails to make sure they tested different angles that included all of the problems he knew the bag could solve, and this is when he began to see an increase in sales. He began to learn the law of mutual exchange and mutual benefit. He let people know his bag could solve the problems that other bags could not, and if the customers were not satisfied, he would offer a full refund and free returns.

One month later, a social media influencer and creator with over fifteen million followers purchased the bag and posted it on her page with no compensation requested. Within twenty-four hours, Paul did roughly $300,000 in sales. To this day, he has created and opened over six highly successful businesses and brands that, in total, accumulate over eight figures in revenue each year.

If Paul had quit, he never would have been in this position. His journey unfolded in divine timing and order. He did not sit around and expect money to fall on his lap. He cultivated a burning desire for it. He began

Mutual Exchange

visualizing himself as the one he desired to be, seeing in his mind's eye the success of his companies before he even began opening them. He was confident in his abilities and overcame his temporary failures. He learned of the power of mutual exchange and mutual benefit. He found the latent powers contained within him that expressed his cosmic will. He committed and persisted toward his definite aim and vision. His effort grew effortless as he began to act according to his cosmic will.

He realized that as long as he thought from his vision, everything would fall into place. He concentrated on his aim and did not bother to get sidetracked. He learned that, in truth, there is no such thing as failure, for his temporary failures led him to change his state of consciousness and tune his frequency to the station of prosperity. The lessons he learned and the knowledge he obtained from his temporary failures are what made the companies he owns today. He learned that in the world of wealth, abundance, and prosperity, there is no such thing as something for nothing. He learned that in order to receive anything from the world, you must first give to the world.

Those who make money without considering the law of mutual exchange and mutual benefit will never be content, fulfilled, or happy. Their money will soon be all they have, and they will eventually be sick of it. The people I speak of are thieves, scammers, robbers, and imposters. Although they think they are happy because of their money, they don't realize that the path they chose is slowly manifesting sickness and mental illness.

Mutual Exchange

Now, they can surely say, "I don't care. I'm happy. I'm making boatloads of money, and that is all I care about," but, in truth, deep down in their heart, they know that they are lying to themselves, for they know that there is always more to be made.

The people who choose this route are the same individuals who believe they are valueless and worthless. Rather than becoming valuable and confident in themselves, they choose a lazy and mentally weak route that manifests anxiety, fear, and paranoia, ultimately resulting in a loss of love, value, trust, character, integrity, and honesty.

People who merely take money from others without giving anything in return operate in a state of lack and inadequacy. Through the repetition of scamming or stealing, they impress their minds with the belief that there is no other way to make money. This belief creates their lives, and they teach their children and loved ones that their way of making money is the only way they make money. This belief gets passed down from generation to generation until someone breaks the cycle and becomes free from this purposeless cage of limitation. Until someone breaks the cycle, the thoughts and opportunities of making money will be limited to stealing or taking it from those who earn it.

If you are one of these people, forgive yourself now and break the cycle. See your innocence in not knowing and not realizing. Trust in your ability to create a prosperous life that will benefit both humanity and yourself. Begin now and change all future generations.

Specialized Knowledge

After all that has been discussed throughout this book so far, one of the most important things one must acquire in order to manifest success on his path to prosperity is specialized knowledge. Specialized knowledge is the quality that allows us to discern right from wrong and think correctly. Not only does it improve our reasoning, but it also creates avenues of possibilities to improve our products or services. Specialized knowledge is needed for those who do not desire the typical average success but the success that influences others and makes a true impact on the world.

Knowledge is power. Not just the typical knowledge we have been taught through traditional education but the specialized knowledge that one must commit to learning in whichever area he has chosen to create prosperity. This type of knowledge I speak of goes beyond mere facts. Specialized knowledge is obtained by those who understand more than the average individual toward a specific area, field, or industry.

The accumulation of specialized knowledge comes from mastering skills and concepts that set one apart from one's chosen endeavor. To serve at a profound level, one must commit to knowing more, knowing better, and applying that knowledge with precision and effectiveness.

Without progressively accumulating specialized knowledge, one can never progressively realize and evolve their vision. If we are relying on someone to do something for us, but we do not know what needs to be

Specialized Knowledge

done, we lose our ability to be in control of our choices and open ourselves up to wrong decisions and mistakes from others.

Specialized knowledge does not pertain to only one particular skill in one particular endeavor. Specialized knowledge pertains to mastering all the skills and understanding the aspects of your endeavor that hold the most value. Those with specialized knowledge intuitively know what needs to be done for their business to thrive and grow, and they either handle it themselves or know how to communicate it effectively. Those without specialized knowledge are unable to find out the exact problem when it arises and, therefore, cannot handle it or even communicate it to someone else. Ultimately, those without specialized knowledge cannot be in full control of their creations. They must rely and depend on an outside source for their success, and since this is the case, the evolution of their service is contingent upon somebody else.

A good home contractor, for example, should wear multiple hats and know about what matters the most. They should know the important things about electricity, plumbing, sheetrock, flooring, etc. If the home contractor knows very little about flooring and relies on someone else to do it with little to no preference or guidance, then his success as a contractor will depend on the one doing the flooring. Ultimately, the home contractor will not be in control of the success of his company, and since he is not progressively learning more about the skills in his field that matter the most, he will only ever see the same results and will not be able to evolve unless he evolves his knowledge.

Specialized Knowledge

You can most certainly rely on others for your success, but know that by so doing your success is dependent upon them. Are there talented individuals who already have specialized knowledge in a particular area? Absolutely, and it is these people that you must find in order to grow and evolve your product or service. Nonetheless, when you yourself have specialized knowledge, you are able to create a mastermind and open yourself up to giving and receiving more and more value, which will inevitably lead to more success.

Say you wish to hire a marketing agency to grow your company, but you know little to nothing about marketing. In this case, you may interview a couple of different agencies. They may all impress you with their millions of dollars in ad spend throughout the companies they have worked with and evolved.

You make the decision to hire one of them after shopping around for a while to see which agency is best for you. You give them a budget, and they get to work. A month in, you see that the agency is not bringing you the desired results. They tell you that the problem is coming from the ads you are giving them to launch, so they request new ones.

Now, you begin looking for a creative agency to create your ads. After some interviews, you find a good agency, give them a budget, and they begin making your ads and sending them to your marketing agency to structure your campaigns and launch your ads.

Specialized Knowledge

A month later, you are still not seeing the results you want to see. The agency that is making your ads is top-notch in the field, and the marketing team that is launching your ads is also top-notch in the field. Rather than the agencies trying to find ways to improve, they begin blaming each other and continue doing what they have been doing without any guidance.

Now, you're stuck. You see the ads that the agency is providing you and the other agency, and you consider them to be good, but in reality, you are not sure because it is not your field, and you are not specialized in breaking down and understanding what actually makes top-performing ads. You see the campaign structure from the other agency you're working with, and you do not know how to read the metrics and break down the analytics. In this instance, there can be many reasons you are not seeing the results you want.

Now, you must make a decision. You must either start looking for new agencies and testing them until you finally find the right one that will give you the results you desire, or you can take the stand and become in total control of your company's growth by beginning to master the skills that you're currently lacking and accumulating the specialized knowledge that is needed for your company to grow and evolve.

Specialized knowledge is not just about knowing one thing; it is about knowing and mastering what matters the most for your growth.

Specialized Knowledge

If you're a salesperson in a commission-based field, you must accumulate as much knowledge as possible in your field so you can provide the best possible service. You must master the skill and art of speaking effectively and efficiently. You must know the trends in your field and influence people to make decisions with ease. You must cultivate the ability to become an extremely good listener and find how you can best serve your client's needs.

If you're in the restaurant business, you must know your recipes and master the craft of food so you can satisfy the hunger of your customers. You must be able to train your employees to provide the best customer service so you can offer a great experience all in all.

If you have an online business, not only do you need to know the ins and outs of the field that you're in, but you also need to know as much as you can about digital marketing. Although physical locations also require marketing as a necessary component of their growth, given that they are in a good location, they can grow and succeed without the need for much digital marketing.

Nonetheless, accumulating marketing knowledge is necessary for any company's evolution, whether physical or online. The success of an online business is subject to the success of its digital marketing. If one chooses to start an online business, one must accumulate as much digital marketing knowledge as possible and cultivate the skills needed to market successfully.

Specialized Knowledge

If there were only one thing I would encourage you to begin accumulating specialized knowledge in, no matter what industry or field you're in, it would be marketing. You can have the best possible product or service that would have the ability to change the entire world, but if you don't know how to advertise it, or if you don't know how to brand it, or if you don't know how to create the best possible offer for it, or if no one is aware of it, it will be rendered lifeless.

Since there is a lot to discuss about marketing, and this book was not intended to learn about marketing, I will not be diving further into the subject; however, no matter what field you're in, the greater you understand the psychology behind advertising and the more you master the skill of marketing, the greater your ability to evolve.

One can take many avenues to create a life of prosperity and live financially free, and specialized knowledge is the key to success no matter which avenue you choose to walk through. The more you learn about your field, the greater your ability to tap into higher levels of thought and unlock correct thinking, which is the intuitive ability to know what needs to be done to evolve.

Specialized knowledge will make you stand out as the confident and intelligent being you are and unlock the control you need for your success. As you continue on your path toward mastering skills and accumulating specialized knowledge, you will naturally transform fear into faith, transmute doubt into trust, and be free from second causes.

Indoctrination

Since childhood, we have been indoctrinated into accepting belief systems that could either serve or harm us. Not only were we taught about what money is, we were also taught where to spend it, how to spend it, how to treat those who have a lot of it and how to treat those who lack it, how to make money, why we make money, how important money is, how capable we are of making money, and what to do with the money we make.

Most, if not all of our beliefs toward money are pervasive and deeply ingrained into our being since we were kids. Our beliefs differ among countries, families, cultures, and people. When we were kids, we accepted everything we were taught as true, and if there are limiting beliefs and attitudes that we have not released and let go of, they are most likely still lingering within our subconscious minds, being expressed automatically without our awareness of their expressions.

Some beliefs are formed due to cultural standards or familial lessons, while others are even reinforced by personal experiences or societal messages. Much of what you were taught about money, whether negative or false, is acceptable by groups worldwide and constantly being projected on the media and in the outer world.

Robert T. Kiyosaki, in his book titled, "Rich Dad, Poor Dad," wrote, "The single most powerful asset we all have is our mind. If it is trained well, it can create enormous wealth." Robert T. Kiyosaki goes on in his book to explain the different belief systems held by the poor and the rich,

Indoctrination

specifically providing insights by contrasting the perspectives of two father figures in his life: his biological father ("Poor Dad") and the father of his childhood best friend ("Rich Dad").

Poor Dad believed in the traditional education system. He emphasized the importance of obtaining good grades and earning a college degree to ensure job security, while Rich Dad, on the other hand, didn't dismiss that idea entirely, but he believed more in the practical learning of financial literacy and education that schools didn't teach.

Poor Dad worked for money, while Rich Dad made money work for him. Poor Dad advocated playing it safe and avoiding risks, fearing the idea of losing money, while at the same time, Rich Dad encouraged taking calculated risks, believing that investing in yourself and your creations are the best investments you could make.

While this merely skims the surface of the varying belief systems between the rich and the poor, it is important to reflect, seek, and understand the belief systems you have been indoctrinated into so you can identify the beliefs that are serving you and the ones that are preventing you from moving forward.

Money is one of the greatest misunderstood concepts throughout the ages, from those who are brought into the world and taught that money is evil to those who are taught to chase after it madly and do anything to get their hands on a couple of bucks. Both belief systems

Indoctrination

are severely wrong and deluded, for it is not money itself that is evil or good, but what the money does. Sure, people do evil things with the money they make, which can create the perspective of money being evil, but people can also do all of the good things in the world with it. It is not the burning desire for money itself that causes one to chase after it madly and do anything for it, regardless of morals, but rather the lack of not having enough. Those who have made money their God are just as ignorant as those who have made it the devil.

Everyone desires money, yes. But it is not money itself that people desire; it is what money can do. Nothing is as necessary as money today to live a happy, content, and whole life. Money means freedom. With money, you are free to give, receive, and do amazing things. You can be fed, clothed, sheltered, and provided with nearly all of the desirable things life has to offer. With money, you can serve more people, create more value, and expand your mastermind. The more money, the more opportunity. The more money, the more freedom.

Before you can cultivate a Wealth Consciousness, you must first release the limiting beliefs preventing you from doing so, whether it be beliefs programmed from the past, created by the present, or directed toward the future. Limiting beliefs will also prevent you from cultivating a deep desire to obtain a Wealth Consciousness. Be aware of the thoughts and feelings arising from your subconscious program. If it does not align with abundance and prosperity, it has to go. It is time to let go. It is time to unbecome.

Part 1

Letting Go

Healing the Subconscious

Wealth Consciousness

$hadow Work

Shadow Work

In this first part of this workbook, you will be guided toward a practice we call "Letting Go." In this part of the workbook, you will be entering the gates of your subconscious and delving into the past environments you were raised in so you can identify the beliefs about money that are serving you, along with the beliefs that are harming you. Subsequently, and as a result, you will be identifying and transcending your present illusory limitations and directing this unlocked potential and level of consciousness toward creating your future.

Essentially, you will be doing a practice that involves what we call shadow work. Shadow work is a process that entails facing and healing your "Shadow," which consists of the subconscious aspects of the ego or personality that have been repressed and neglected. The Shadow contains both positive and negative aspects of the ego, and unless we are conscious of these aspects of our ego, they will be hidden and subconsciously expressed. The shadow derives from the philosophies of Carl Jung, a famous Swiss philosopher and psychologist.

The shadow is expressed beneath our conscious awareness. It encompasses hidden programs that often drive and govern our automatic reactions. It contains the aspect of our ego mind that we may not be ready to acknowledge or want to understand, so we leave them unfaced and allow them to control how we think, feel, and behave. It's a repository of all we reject, despise of, and judge, manifesting in moments of reactivity where our deeper, unexamined feelings emerge to create our perspectives and, thus, our reality.

Shadow Work

However, it would be an oversimplification to label the shadow as merely a reservoir of negativity. Surely, the shadow does not only contain negative aspects of the ego, such as suppressed fears and insecurities, but it also contains positive aspects of the ego, such as hidden talents, forgotten strengths, and untapped potential. Your shadow can and will most likely contain the wisdom and strength required to create an abundant life filled with success and prosperity. It can harbor the very essence of the unacknowledged brilliance potent within you, waiting to be recognized and fully expressed.

The shadow could cause one to unconsciously underestimate themselves and their abilities and neglect their true worth and potential alongside their true desires and expressions. For example, someone might choose a stable 9-5 job because it's socially acceptable, or maybe it was the only way they were taught it was the only acceptable way they could make money from their childhood, even if they currently have an entrepreneurial spirit that could lead them to start a successful business or a hidden talent that could lead them to unlock new doors of opportunity. The shadow, in this instance, manifests a deep-seated belief that they aren't capable or deserving of doing anything other than what they were taught was right for them.

As long as the shadow remains hidden, it will be expressed automatically without our awareness. It will control and govern our thoughts, behaviors, and emotions, and we will call it fate. Everything we neglect and suppress, we do so out of fear, whether it be the fear of

Letting Go

judgments, societal pressures, or our childhood environments. When we are brainwashed by our childhood indoctrination and influenced by society's expectations, we are dissuaded from taking risks, being who we truly desire to be, and doing what we genuinely desire to do.

If you wish to break free from this unconscious cage of limitation, you must cultivate a willingness to face your past life experiences with innocence, love, compassion, forgiveness, strength, and power so you can consciously create the life you have so long been searching for and unlock the latent powers hidden within you.

You are the Creator of your reality. Choose now to shine the light on the darkness by becoming conscious of the unconscious. Let go and release the aspects of your shadow that are no longer serving you, and unlock the hidden powers from the aspects waiting to be acknowledged and accepted. Earnestly and deliberately take conscious control over your reality, or your shadow will take control for you.

Remember that your true self is beyond all. Your true self is I AM. For as long as you remember this, you will remember your powers to create, and you will be able to create anything you wish, whenever you wish, as you wish. Do not merely think of creation as what you see in the outside world. Your creation is the very self that has thought and felt itself into being, the very self that has not only been created by you but by your outer world since birth. I tell you now, you are and will forever be greater than your creation, for you are the Creator of it all.

Letting Go

Tuning your frequency to the station of wealth is synonymous with reprogramming your mind to the state of wealth. In order to reprogram your subconscious mind, you must first begin by being lovingly aware of what lies therein, to which you identify what serves you and what doesn't, what is suppressed and neglected, and what is waiting to be acknowledged and expressed.

Letting go goes beyond simply letting go of the past. It involves letting go of all of the thoughts, feelings, and behaviors that have deluded your assumptions toward your future and have dirtied the lens through which you view yourself and your world in this very present moment.

The upcoming practice of shadow work and letting go will aid you in doing this. I endeavor to have the following practice: (1) heal your past, (2) shift your perspective of the present, and (3) change your assumptions toward your future.

You will start by answering questions about money and wealth from your past. These questions will cause you to identify hidden subconscious thoughts, feelings, emotions, and beliefs about money that may have been programmed since childhood and either neglected or suppressed. It is wise that you answer these questions honestly. There is no point in lying because you would only be lying to yourself if you were to do so. Take your time with certain questions if you need.

Letting Go

When reflecting on your past, withhold any urges that may cause you to blame someone or something, whether it be an experience or even yourself. You are the creator of your reality; you are not a victim of it. You must reflect on your past with an earnest intention to transcend beyond the limitations created by it. Answer the questions with innocence by realizing you were brought into the world and did not have a choice but to innocently accept what you were taught. See the innocence in others by realizing that they have also been innocently indoctrinated in the same way. Forgive yourself and forgive them, for you did not know the truth, and they did not know what they accepted as the truth.

Afterward, you will come across questions about your current perspective on money. After reading this book and completing the prompts provided for the section on the past, you will already experience a shift in your perspective toward money. However, be sure to answer the questions as honestly as possible so you can identify anything else lingering in the subconscious that may be waiting to be acknowledged.

Lastly, you will be directed toward identifying the perspectives and assumptions you hold toward your future. Adhere to the same set of preceding rules and identify your current expectations for the future. When answering the questions, practice visualizing and feeling. Be free to write anything that comes to your mind with innocence. Be ready to heal, forgive, release, let go, and evolve.

I NOW RELEASE THE LIMITING BELIEFS PREVENTING ME FROM REALIZING MY ABUNDANT WORTH.

Past

Healing Your Past

Answer Honestly

Acknowledge the Past

Identify the Lessons Taught

Create Positive Affirmations

Forgive Self and Others

Release and Let Go

Visualize Your Ideal

What beliefs did people hold about money growing up?
Have these beliefs influenced me?

_____

_____

_____

_____

_____

_____

_____

_____

_____

_____

_____

_____

What would I say to my younger self?

_____

_____

_____

_____

_____

_____

_____

_____

_____

_____

_____

_____

_____

When was the last time I made a financial mistake?
What did you learn?

_____

_____

_____

_____

_____

_____

_____

_____

_____

_____

_____

_____

What has shaped my perception of financial risk?

_____

_____

_____

_____

_____

_____

_____

_____

_____

_____

_____

_____

_____

Who has had the most influence on me toward money?

_____

_____

_____

_____

_____

_____

_____

_____

_____

_____

_____

_____

Did I grow up in a strict spending environment?
Has it influenced my spending?

_____

_____

_____

_____

_____

_____

_____

_____

_____

_____

_____

_____

_____

Present

Your Current Position

Answer Honestly

Visualize Your Days

Control Your Breathing

Create Positive Affirmations

Take Your Attention Away From the World

Disregard Your Rational Reasoning Mind

Feel Yourself Being Transformed

Concentrate on Your Aim

Create Consciously

What are my current beliefs toward financial success?

_____

_____

_____

_____

_____

_____

_____

_____

_____

_____

_____

What impact does my environment have on me?

_____

_____

_____

_____

_____

_____

_____

_____

_____

_____

_____

_____

_____

_____

What habits are influencing my ability to make money?

_____

_____

_____

_____

_____

_____

_____

_____

_____

_____

_____

_____

_____

How confident am I in my ability to make money?

_____

_____

_____

_____

_____

_____

_____

_____

_____

_____

_____

How can I serve others with my purpose?

_____

_____

_____

_____

_____

_____

_____

_____

_____

_____

_____

_____

Is anything preventing me from taking action?

_____

_____

_____

_____

_____

_____

_____

_____

_____

_____

_____

_____

Future

Creating Your Future

Have Faith

Concentrate

Be Determined

Move in Silence

Visualize Your Ideal

Take Deliberate Action

Create Positive Affirmations

Make Your Future a Present Fact

What are my assumptions toward the future?

_____

_____

_____

_____

_____

_____

_____

_____

_____

_____

_____

How would I feel if I was financially free?

_____

_____

_____

_____

_____

_____

_____

_____

_____

_____

_____

_____

What would I do if failure wasn't an option?

_____

_____

_____

_____

_____

_____

_____

_____

_____

_____

_____

Where do I see myself financially in 5, 10, and 20 years?

_____

_____

_____

_____

_____

_____

_____

_____

_____

_____

_____

_____

What does my financially free life look like?

_____

_____

_____

_____

_____

_____

_____

_____

_____

_____

_____

_____

How do I see my relationship with money evolving?

_____

_____

_____

_____

_____

_____

_____

_____

_____

_____

_____

_____

_____

_____

Part 2

Reprogramming

Auto-Suggestion

Are you ready to accept riches?

Reprogramming

In this section of the workbook, I will aspire to have your subconscious mind reprogrammed through the power and force of conscious autosuggestion. Essentially, you will be required to repetitively and deliberately suggest affirmations to *your self* by *your Self*.

A suggestion creates an impression upon the mind, whether it be a suggestion coming from an experience, someone else, or yourself. We are constantly accepting or rejecting suggestions based on our state of consciousness and the degree of truth contained within the suggestion.

In order for you to recognize the possibilities that can be unlocked through the use of autosuggestion, you must first bring your attention to the two aspects of your mind: your *conscious mind* and your *subconscious mind*. Your conscious mind is the active mind that voluntarily makes decisions. Your subconscious mind is the passive mind that recreates or reproduces what the conscious mind has already created through programmed memory.

Your conscious mind is the aspect of the mind that can either accept or deny a suggestion. It is the mind that manifests the will and is primarily used when we are focusing or concentrating. Our subconscious mind, on the other hand, is the mind that manifests in ways contrary to the conscious mind. The subconscious mind performs actions automatically, exhibiting little to no will or effort.

The subconscious mind is your most valuable servant, as it takes care

Reprogramming

of the actions previously performed and programmed by the conscious mind effortlessly. When done persistently, actions that primarily take conscious effort will inevitably manifest into effortless action. I aim to prove this concept and have you manifest its latent powers by the end of this workbook, where we will discuss the concept of Effortless Action more thoroughly and manifest it through our Cosmic Will.

The subconscious mind not only performs effortless action; it also performs effortless thinking, effortless feeling, and effortless expression, which can also be perceived as automatic reactivity.

Most people in the world do not want to think consciously, feel consciously, or be conscious of their expressions; they prefer the comfortable and effortless route of expressing their past program automatically with little to no effort or will, even if their program is harming them or making them depressed. The very nature of not exercising the will consciously makes one mentally lazy and desireless.

Those who continually think the same thoughts, do the same things and feel the same way have most likely not been conscious or exercised their will for a considerable amount of time. Hence, they would be living in a program. If you have not been conscious of the suggestions that are constantly surrounding you, your subconscious mind will solely reaffirm and reproduce more of what has already been suggested from the past, and it will do so until you consciously suggest new possibilities through thought, feeling, and action.

Reprogramming

In the morning, you will be reading and asserting affirmations in the form of autosuggestion as follows: Your highest self, which we have called the "I AM" part of you, will suggest the affirmations provided to the "me" side of you, which is your personality. Another way you can perceive it is your conscious mind asserting the affirmations provided to your subconscious mind. Thereafter, you will be writing nine of your own affirmations in the corresponding lines below the provided autosuggestions. At night, you will answer the prompts on the following page, respectively.

A meditative state is encouraged. Sit in a comfortable position, close your eyes, and direct your attention inward, away from the outer world. Relax every part of your body until it is completely loose. Enter into the stillness of the Unconditioned Mind by silencing your thoughts and keeping your attention on the present moment. If thoughts arise, gently catch your attention and bring it back to the presence of your breath. Do this until your body and mind are still.

Once a meditative state is reached, bring your attention to the affirmations provided. Read the suggestions, accept them as true, and write nine of your own affirmations. When writing your additional affirmations, ensure they are in harmony with your financial goals and aims. An example of some affirmations would be: "I am effortlessly making $20,000 a month. I am constantly receiving opportunities to make money. I take action on all of my ideas. There is no idea too big for me. I sold 100,000 units this month."

Reprogramming

We encourage you to be as specific as possible while not limiting yourself to the infinite possibilities awaiting to be suggested, accepted, and ultimately expressed. The affirmations you write are yours to feel and believe as true of yourself and your world. Failure to accept our suggestions and deliberately write your own may cause a shift in mental attitude. As a result, you may treat these practices as an obligation or chore, which can cause you to deny our suggestions with disbelief or ridicule. Such behavior will create negative impressions and prevent you from obtaining a Wealth Consciousness.

Once you finish the exercises in the morning, visualize and feel yourself acting on the following suggestions and affirmations. Visualize yourself possessing the qualities suggested and affirmed. Imagine the money entering your bank account, the successful launch of a new business, the purchase of your dream home or car, or the manifestation of a desired outcome that reflects your financial desires.

The more you occupy yourself mentally with the reality of wealth, and the longer you maintain the theater in your mind's eye, the quicker you will tune your frequency to the station of wealth and reprogram your subconscious mind. It is encouraged to train your imagination, for by doing so, you are exercising your will and creating consciously. Your imagination is like a muscle that should be exercised every day.

After you visualize, align yourself with your goal or aim by concentrating on it to the best of your ability. Think from your vision,

Reprogramming

doing what you would be doing, thinking as you would be thinking, feeling as you would be feeling, and being as you would be were you to be living the life you envisioned, here and now.

Block out and reject any and all suggestions not in alignment with the affirmations you have read and written. Do not only impress but also express our suggestions along with your affirmations throughout the day. If someone suggests something that contradicts our suggestions, disregard it while staying true to yourself. Keep our suggestions and your affirmations private, for others are merely limited only to their own perceptions and suggestions toward you. However, their suggestions will inevitably converge with yours over time.

If your physical reality is not in alignment with our suggestions and your affirmations, take your attention away from your current position in physical reality and bring it inward. Deny your outer world and remove all of its power by recognizing that you are the creator of it, not the other way around. Realize that the manifestation of your outer world is the effect of your mind, and by deliberately changing your mind, you will deliberately change your world.

If your outer world presents something deemed as evidence contrary to the suggestions and affirmations, understand the outer world is merely reflecting a past program, a past state of consciousness, a past suggestion that has been innocently accepted, and your outer world has only to catch up to your reconditioned Wealth Consciousness.

Reprogramming

If negative thoughts or suggestions pop up in your awareness, deny them, not by thinking or feeling that you are not the suggestion, but by thinking and feeling a positive suggestion that counteracts and neutralizes the negative suggestion.

As day turns to night, prior to going to sleep, address the three prompts on the following page: "Why do I deserve a wealthy life? How do I visualize myself living a wealthy life? How do I feel knowing that I am wealthy?"

While I could dive extensively into the rationale and reasoning behind my selection of these questions and the importance of answering them, I'll assume that it is not needed and simply highlight that answering them with integrity and accepting your answers as your truth instills the conviction of your prosperity, wealth, and abundance.

Ensure that you do not sidetrack yourself after you answer the prompts provided. Your answers should be your final thoughts before falling asleep. This is crucial due to the state that you are in before going to sleep, as it is the state that enables you to enter the gates of your subconscious mind and impress it with ease.

Adhere to this routine for 30 consecutive days. Amidst your morning and evening practices, I encourage you to go back and reread the contents of the book regularly, and believe me when I tell you, you're already rich. The work is done. It is time for you to accept it now.

888

The Universe is creating an infinite number of avenues for money to enter your life. It is time for you to accept it. Multiple revenue streams are becoming available to you now. It is all happening for you now. Everything is aligned.

Nine Affirmations

_____

_____

_____

_____

_____

_____

_____

_____

___/___/___

Why do I deserve a wealthy life?

_____

_____

_____

_____

How do I visualize myself living a wealthy life?

_____

_____

_____

_____

How do I feel knowing that I am wealthy?

_____

_____

_____

_____

333

You're a smart and hard worker. It doesn't take effort for you to make money. You do it effortlessly because you are a wealthy being. You take pleasure in your financial independence. You are paid in abundance. You are financially free.

Nine Affirmations

_____

_____

_____

_____

_____

_____

_____

_____

___/___/___

Why do I deserve a wealthy life?

_____

_____

_____

_____

How do I visualize myself living a wealthy life?

_____

_____

_____

_____

How do I feel knowing that I am wealthy?

_____

_____

_____

_____

1111

You always have more than enough. You are independent and able to afford all that you need. It seems as though whatever you pay for comes back multiplied. You never worry because you're always grateful for everything you have.

Nine Affirmations

_____

_____

_____

_____

_____

_____

_____

_____

_____

__/__/__

Why do I deserve a wealthy life?

_____

_____

_____

_____

How do I visualize myself living a wealthy life?

_____

_____

_____

_____

How do I feel knowing that I am wealthy?

_____

_____

_____

_____

222

Your life is abundant. It's like everywhere you look, you are surrounded by an ample supply of money. You are continuously receiving a surplus of abundance and prosperity. Possibilities are being presented in every direction you turn.

Nine Affirmations

_____

_____

_____

_____

_____

_____

_____

_____

_____

___ / ___ / ___

Why do I deserve a wealthy life?

_____

_____

_____

_____

How do I visualize myself living a wealthy life?

_____

_____

_____

_____

How do I feel knowing that I am wealthy?

_____

_____

_____

_____

999

You are beginning to find it easier and more simple to obtain wealth. You have an amazing natural ability to earn and attract money as you please, whenever you please. Prosperity is effortlessly flowing into your life. You are successful in all you attempt.

Nine Affirmations

_____

_____

_____

_____

_____

_____

_____

_____

__/__/__

Why do I deserve a wealthy life?

_____

_____

_____

_____

How do I visualize myself living a wealthy life?

_____

_____

_____

How do I feel knowing that I am wealthy?

_____

_____

_____

777

You are beginning to understand that there are no limitations to how much money you can make. You are realizing that nothing outside of you has control. You are creating every experience, and are now choosing how much money you allow into your life. You will forever be financially free.

Nine Affirmations

_____

_____

_____

_____

_____

_____

_____

_____

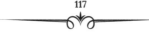

___/___/___

Why do I deserve a wealthy life?

_____

_____

_____

_____

How do I visualize myself living a wealthy life?

_____

_____

_____

_____

How do I feel knowing that I am wealthy?

_____

_____

_____

_____

111

You feel the dormant forces paving the way for wealth to enter your life now. You are finding new doors of opportunity and opening them. You are happily receiving it all. You are welcoming wealth with a gracious mind and a grateful heart. You now realize that everything you want is already yours.

Nine Affirmations

_____

_____

_____

_____

_____

_____

_____

_____

_____

___/___/___

Why do I deserve a wealthy life?

_____

_____

_____

_____

How do I visualize myself living a wealthy life?

_____

_____

_____

_____

How do I feel knowing that I am wealthy?

_____

_____

_____

_____

444

You are witnessing your life flourish with an abundance of riches. All your needs are being fulfilled, and you're getting everything you want. You're believing that everyone can be wealthy and attract abundance like you. You're inspiring those around you to create a prosperous life.

Nine Affirmations

_____

_____

_____

_____

_____

_____

_____

_____

_____

___/___/___

Why do I deserve a wealthy life?

_____

_____

_____

_____

How do I visualize myself living a wealthy life?

_____

_____

_____

_____

How do I feel knowing that I am wealthy?

_____

_____

_____

_____

333

You are now generating wealth for yourself and your family. You're understanding on a deeper level how you can serve others and make money and are willing to teach others. You are understanding your worth and your value in all that you do, and you are getting paid accordingly.

Nine Affirmations

_____

_____

_____

_____

_____

_____

_____

_____

_____

___/___/___

Why do I deserve a wealthy life?

_____

_____

_____

_____

How do I visualize myself living a wealthy life?

_____

_____

_____

_____

How do I feel knowing that I am wealthy?

_____

_____

_____

_____

777

You're managing your money brilliantly. You're enjoying investing in yourself and realizing that it always pays off. You're trusting yourself. You are cultivating the skill of having money flowing passively. Money is being attracted to you easily and is staying with you for a long time.

Nine Affirmations

_____

_____

_____

_____

_____

_____

_____

_____

_____

__/__/__

Why do I deserve a wealthy life?

_____

_____

_____

_____

How do I visualize myself living a wealthy life?

_____

_____

_____

_____

How do I feel knowing that I am wealthy?

_____

_____

_____

_____

555

You're creating wealth on a quantum level. You're manifesting money just by thinking about money. You're beginning to imagine your life the way you want it to be and creating it as such. Every day, you are learning more and more about prosperity.

Nine Affirmations

_____

_____

_____

_____

_____

_____

_____

_____

_____

__/__/__

Why do I deserve a wealthy life?

_____

_____

_____

_____

How do I visualize myself living a wealthy life?

_____

_____

_____

_____

How do I feel knowing that I am wealthy?

_____

_____

_____

_____

888

You're dancing the dance of creation and reaching higher states of consciousness. You are reaching a place where there are no limitations, and as a result, you are attracting more and more wealth. I AM proud of you for all that you are and do.

Nine Affirmations

_____

_____

_____

_____

_____

_____

_____

_____

_____

___/___/___

Why do I deserve a wealthy life?

_____

_____

_____

_____

How do I visualize myself living a wealthy life?

_____

_____

_____

_____

How do I feel knowing that I am wealthy?

_____

_____

_____

_____

222

You're cultivating and embodying all of the thoughts, emotions, and behaviors necessary to live an abundant, wealthy, and prosperous life. Everyone around you is affirming the amount of money you are able to generate. They are realizing how amazing your skills and abilities really are.

Nine Affirmations

_____

_____

_____

_____

_____

_____

_____

_____

__/__/__

Why do I deserve a wealthy life?

_____

_____

_____

_____

How do I visualize myself living a wealthy life?

_____

_____

_____

_____

How do I feel knowing that I am wealthy?

_____

_____

_____

_____

999

Cash is flowing rapidly into your life. You're managing all of your cash flow efficiently and with ease. You are always obtaining more than enough, and expressing gratitude daily for the life you have created for yourself and your loved ones.

Nine Affirmations

_____

_____

_____

_____

_____

_____

_____

_____

——/——/——

Why do I deserve a wealthy life?

_____

_____

_____

_____

How do I visualize myself living a wealthy life?

_____

_____

_____

_____

How do I feel knowing that I am wealthy?

_____

_____

_____

_____

333

You are wealthy, abundant, rich, and powerful because you are unafraid of it. You are not afraid of what others think about you. You realize that what others think about you is only a reflection of the limiting beliefs they have within themselves. You know that you have no limiting beliefs.

Nine Affirmations

_____

_____

_____

_____

_____

_____

_____

_____

_____

___/___/___

Why do I deserve a wealthy life?

_____

_____

_____

_____

How do I visualize myself living a wealthy life?

_____

_____

_____

_____

How do I feel knowing that I am wealthy?

_____

_____

_____

_____

1111

You are finding ways of spending money to make money. You're entertaining your happiness along with your important expenses. You realize that your money is always in circulation and never going to waste. Spending money puts you in an ideal state, allowing more money into your life.

Nine Affirmations

_____

_____

_____

_____

_____

_____

_____

_____

___/___/___

Why do I deserve a wealthy life?

_____

_____

_____

_____

How do I visualize myself living a wealthy life?

_____

_____

_____

_____

How do I feel knowing that I am wealthy?

_____

_____

_____

_____

777

Money is entering your life in different ways. Your savings are rapidly increasing day by day. You're filling your mind with million-dollar ideas and realizing more of your ability to manifest them easily. You are now tapped into the station of wealth. You are now ready to receive.

Nine Affirmations

_____

_____

_____

_____

_____

_____

_____

_____

___/___/___

Why do I deserve a wealthy life?

_____

_____

_____

_____

How do I visualize myself living a wealthy life?

_____

_____

_____

_____

How do I feel knowing that I am wealthy?

_____

_____

_____

_____

999

You are surrounding yourself with wealthy people. They love being around you. They love the energy you give off. You are in alignment with all of the wealthy people in the world. You do not chase them; you attract them. You collaborate with them all the time and celebrate each other's success.

Nine Affirmations

_____

_____

_____

_____

_____

_____

_____

_____

_____

___/___/___

Why do I deserve a wealthy life?

_____

_____

_____

_____

How do I visualize myself living a wealthy life?

_____

_____

_____

_____

How do I feel knowing that I am wealthy?

_____

_____

_____

_____

444

You have a waiting list of people wanting to invest with you. They trust in you. They trust that you are valuable. They inspire you to do better. They know what you bring to the table. They know what you are capable of. They affirm what you already know to be true about yourself.

Nine Affirmations

_____

_____

_____

_____

_____

_____

_____

_____

_____

___/___/___

Why do I deserve a wealthy life?

_____
_____
_____
_____

How do I visualize myself living a wealthy life?

_____
_____
_____
_____

How do I feel knowing that I am wealthy?

_____
_____
_____
_____

888

You're surrounding yourself with people who inspire you. You're continuously networking with wealthy and successful people. They are casually reaffirming all of your truths. They acknowledge who you are and affirm where you're going. You are blessed to have such people surrounding you.

Nine Affirmations

_____

_____

_____

_____

_____

_____

_____

_____

___/___/___

Why do I deserve a wealthy life?

_____

_____

_____

_____

How do I visualize myself living a wealthy life?

_____

_____

_____

_____

How do I feel knowing that I am wealthy?

_____

_____

_____

_____

333

You are creating the life of your dreams. Your world is overflowing with peace, love, wealth, and happiness. You are financially free. You are at peace. You are surrounded by love. You are happy. You're making an impact.

Nine Affirmations

_____

_____

_____

_____

_____

_____

_____

_____

_____

___/___/___

Why do I deserve a wealthy life?

_____

_____

_____

_____

How do I visualize myself living a wealthy life?

_____

_____

_____

_____

How do I feel knowing that I am wealthy?

_____

_____

_____

_____

999

You're realizing that manifesting a wealthy and prosperous life is not hard at all. Whatever amount of money you think you can make is the amount of money you are able to make. You believe that there are no limits to how much money you can make.

Nine Affirmations

_____

_____

_____

_____

_____

_____

_____

_____

_____

___ / ___ / ___

Why do I deserve a wealthy life?

_____

_____

_____

_____

How do I visualize myself living a wealthy life?

_____

_____

_____

_____

How do I feel knowing that I am wealthy?

_____

_____

_____

_____

222

You are aligned with the frequency of wealth and prosperity. The frequency you have tuned your station to attracts opportunities and million-dollar ideas with ease. You're always inspired to create new ways to serve others. The Universe is doing all it can to make you rich. You are ready to receive.

Nine Affirmations

_____

_____

_____

_____

_____

_____

_____

_____

_____

___/___/___

Why do I deserve a wealthy life?

_____

_____

_____

_____

How do I visualize myself living a wealthy life?

_____

_____

_____

_____

How do I feel knowing that I am wealthy?

_____

_____

_____

_____

555

You have everything you've ever wanted. You only see one financial outcome in your life, and that is being financially free. You're expressing your deepest gratitude for what is already yours. You are at peace with what was and have transcended beyond all of the illusory limitations.

Nine Affirmations

_____

_____

_____

_____

_____

_____

_____

_____

___/___/___

Why do I deserve a wealthy life?

_____

_____

_____

_____

How do I visualize myself living a wealthy life?

_____

_____

_____

_____

How do I feel knowing that I am wealthy?

_____

_____

_____

_____

111

You're realizing that nothing is able to limit you from creating a prosperous life and reaching financial freedom. You trust that you know what you're doing. You're certain about your plans. Your plans are being manifested now.

Nine Affirmations

_____

_____

_____

_____

_____

_____

_____

_____

___/___/___

Why do I deserve a wealthy life?

_____

_____

_____

_____

How do I visualize myself living a wealthy life?

_____

_____

_____

_____

How do I feel knowing that I am wealthy?

_____

_____

_____

_____

444

You have always assumed that you were going to be wealthy one day. Now, you can see the evidence. Everything you have imagined is being created. The contents of your consciousness are being projected right in front of you, and so far, it is greater than you imagined. It's already done.

Nine Affirmations

_____
_____
_____
_____
_____
_____
_____
_____
_____

___/___/___

Why do I deserve a wealthy life?

_____

_____

_____

_____

How do I visualize myself living a wealthy life?

_____

_____

_____

_____

How do I feel knowing that I am wealthy?

_____

_____

_____

_____

888

You are starting to live your life from a new perspective, where you can choose to create any life you desire. You're learning how to attract anything with ease. You're realizing your abundant worth and actualizing your purpose.

Nine Affirmations

_____

_____

_____

_____

_____

_____

_____

_____

_____

___/___/___

Why do I deserve a wealthy life?

_____

_____

_____

_____

How do I visualize myself living a wealthy life?

_____

_____

_____

_____

How do I feel knowing that I am wealthy?

_____

_____

_____

_____

999

Everywhere you go, you radiate abundance. Every single day you are being showered with more than you could ever ask for. You're trusting the process and knowing that everything you're going through is happening for you to receive your wealth.

Nine Affirmations

_____

_____

_____

_____

_____

_____

_____

_____

___/___/___

Why do I deserve a wealthy life?

_____

_____

_____

_____

How do I visualize myself living a wealthy life?

_____

_____

_____

_____

How do I feel knowing that I am wealthy?

_____

_____

_____

_____

222

You're understanding that wealth goes far beyond mere currency. You're deeply appreciating all of the wisdom and knowledge you are gaining and have gained on your journey toward creating prosperity. You're loving the journey.

Nine Affirmations

_____

_____

_____

_____

_____

_____

_____

_____

_____

___/___/___

Why do I deserve a wealthy life?

_____

_____

_____

_____

How do I visualize myself living a wealthy life?

_____

_____

_____

_____

How do I feel knowing that I am wealthy?

_____

_____

_____

_____

111

Everywhere you go, you carry an innate magnetism that draws all of the people, places, and things necessary for prosperity to enter your life. You're finding yourself surrounded by golden opportunities as each day passes by.

Nine Affirmations

_____

_____

_____

_____

_____

_____

_____

_____

_____

___/___/___

Why do I deserve a wealthy life?

_____

_____

_____

_____

How do I visualize myself living a wealthy life?

_____

_____

_____

_____

How do I feel knowing that I am wealthy?

_____

_____

_____

_____

Part 3

Effortless Action

The Cosmic Will

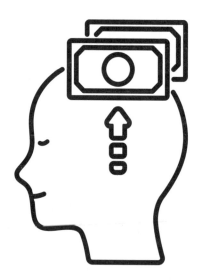

I CAN I CAN I CAN I CAN I CAN I CAN I CAN I CAN I CAN I CAN
I WILL I WILL I WILL I WILL I WILL I WILL I WILL I WILL I WILL I WILL

I CAN I CAN I CAN I CAN I CAN I CAN I CAN I CAN I CAN I CAN
I WILL I WILL I WILL I WILL I WILL I WILL I WILL I WILL I WILL I WILL

I CAN I CAN I CAN I CAN I CAN I CAN I CAN I CAN I CAN I CAN
I WILL I WILL I WILL I WILL I WILL I WILL I WILL I WILL I WILL I WILL

I CAN I CAN I CAN I CAN I CAN I CAN I CAN I CAN I CAN I CAN
I WILL I WILL I WILL I WILL I WILL I WILL I WILL I WILL I WILL I WILL

I CAN I CAN I CAN I CAN I CAN I CAN I CAN I CAN I CAN I CAN
I WILL I WILL I WILL I WILL I WILL I WILL I WILL I WILL I WILL I WILL

I CAN I CAN I CAN I CAN I CAN I CAN I CAN I CAN I CAN I CAN
I WILL I WILL I WILL I WILL I WILL I WILL I WILL I WILL I WILL I WILL

I CAN I CAN I CAN I CAN I CAN I CAN I CAN I CAN I CAN I CAN
I WILL I WILL I WILL I WILL I WILL I WILL I WILL I WILL I WILL I WILL

I CAN I CAN I CAN I CAN I CAN I CAN I CAN I CAN I CAN I CAN
I WILL I WILL I WILL I WILL I WILL I WILL I WILL I WILL I WILL I WILL

I CAN I CAN I CAN I CAN I CAN I CAN I CAN I CAN I CAN I CAN
I WILL I WILL I WILL I WILL I WILL I WILL I WILL I WILL I WILL I WILL

I CAN I CAN I CAN I CAN I CAN I CAN I CAN I CAN I CAN I CAN
I WILL I WILL I WILL I WILL I WILL I WILL I WILL I WILL I WILL I WILL

The Cosmic Will

As you now stand at the cusp of obtaining a Wealth Consciousness, we shall direct your attention to the final part of our workbook. Here, you will discover how to express and manifest your reconditioned consciousness into Effortless Action through your Cosmic Will.

Without the expression of the mind manifested by the will, this book would serve no purpose. We have already guided you through the following stages: (1) Healing the Unconscious Shadow by becoming conscious of the unconscious; identifying beliefs that no longer serve you, releasing negatives, and embracing the positives from the past, present, and future through acknowledgment, visualization, forgiveness, love, power, and optimism. (2) Reprogramming the Subconscious Mind through Conscious Auto-Suggestion; feeling and accepting suggestions in vibrational alignment with the lifestyles and minds of the wealthy and prosperous, that of which are made by the "I" and accepted by the "me." Additionally, responding to prompts that further support a wealth consciousness.

The will is the last and final process required for the manifestation and expression of the mind in action. The will is now primed and ready to be manifested through decision (determined choice) and voluntary action (conscious manifestation).

If you have begun taking action toward your aim, I commend and encourage you to persist and persevere, assuring that you are on the right path toward creating a life of success and prosperity. If you have

The Cosmic Will

not begun taking a course of action, it could be by cause of (a) lack of a goal or aim, often expressed as "not knowing what to do or where to start," (b) lack of desire, or (c) lack of faith or confidence.

In order for the will to manifest the expression of the mind, the mind must first have an aim or goal. We have already uncovered the broader aim, which is, in this instance, financial freedom. However, remember that financial freedom and money itself are results, not causes. The money we earn is proportional to the value we provide. Without value, there is no offer, and without an offer, there is no money.

If you're unsure of where to begin or what to do to create financial prosperity, and if you do not have a particular aim to act upon, it's likely due to your perception of the process of creating prosperity. Money is manifested as a result of serving others. As we focus our attention more upon what we can serve and how we can serve, simply for the joy of serving rather than solely for money, the possibilities of serving others will flow to us and through us effortlessly in abundance, leading to countless avenues of prosperity and service.

Rather than thinking of what you can do to make money, think of what you can offer that will serve others. Until you have found and created the best possible offer you can, your aim should be your offer, and you should have no other aims in view, ensuring your full attention is directed toward creating ways to maximize the value of your offer. As you continue thinking this way, you will have no problem finding aims.

The Cosmic Will

If you take a moment now and ask yourself in reflection, "Do I desire to create prosperity?" You will most likely find your answer to be yes. I mean, let us consider that you have acquired this book and have made it this far, which means that, of course, you desire to create prosperity.

The question arises, "How strongly do I desire to create financial freedom?" You see, about 99% of people want to make money, but only a few percent of those people who "want it" WANT IT hard enough. The people who do want it hard enough activate their cosmic will and manifest their entire willpower to ensure financial security and independence. They are purposeful and determined to do so with confident expectations and will not be sidetracked by anything that is not their aim, while those who want money just as a mere wish and do not want it hard enough to do what it takes to create a life of prosperity will not be able to cultivate a Wealth Consciousness, for it is that very mental attitude that prevents the will from being expressed.

When you want something hard enough, forces beyond regular means are activated, and your Cosmic Will manifests into Persistent Determination, also known as Commitment. This occurs when one finally desires hard enough and is willing to sacrifice and pay the price for its attainment, such as building the intense burning desire to release an attachment or quit an addiction that has long been serving as a predominant desire.

Your Cosmic will is unlocked automatically with the recognition of the

The Cosmic Will

I AM within you, aka your unconditioned consciousness, the Creator. We have merely skimmed upon the surface of the powers of I AM and its relation to wealth and prosperity at the beginning of the book, but for the purpose of unlocking our cosmic will, we deem it necessary to go deeper into manifesting its latent and dormant powers.

There is but one I AM that exists, and you are the individualization and extension of this one I AM. With this realization, understand that the same power that created this Universe lies dormant within you, beyond your reasoning and far beyond the logical and conditioned mind of the "me" that holds your current beliefs.

We have heard of the mother lifting a car to save her trapped child. One could make the claim that the mother was genuinely strong, but such claims would be ignorant of the truth. Where did she get this power? Where did she get this force? If it cannot be from the conditioned beliefs of the mother, it must only mean that there was a force or power beyond her. It must only mean that there was a Cosmic Will beyond her regular will that was manifested. It was the Cosmic Will of her I AM rather than the will of her "me" that was unlocked through her intense burning desire to save her child.

You will to do what you will to do because you will to be who you will to be. If you were to recognize the truth of who you are, everything, including your will to be and your will to do, would change.

The Cosmic Will

Those who believe they are the "me" of their personality will forever be limited to the powers and qualities held in that particular personality. There is more than enough evidence proving the infinite storehouse of Cosmic Willpower dormant within you. There is a Cosmic Will far beyond what the will of the personality or ego is capable of, and it is unlocked through an intense burning desire.

I tell you again, the power of the Cosmic Will exists in you, and it is manifested through the recognition of the I AM that is beyond who you believe you are. Unlocking it will not only aid you in your path toward creating prosperity but in everything you do in life. Look beyond the conditioned I AM of my name, my body, my personality, my beliefs, my thoughts, my feelings, my actions and find the infinite unconditioned creator of it all: "I AM." Recognize the infinite possibilities contained within the one I AM and choose wisely the suggestions of the possibilities you wish to create for yourself, realizing that you are here as the Creator, and you, as the Creator, will forever be greater than all of your creations.

Now, if you have an aim, and you have cultivated a burning desire for it, but you just can't seem to activate your will to take action on it due to a lack of faith or confidence, you have still yet to release the fears and worries of the "me" that are preventing you from moving forward and manifesting your will in action. If you were to realize the I AM within you, all fear and worry-based thoughts and beliefs would dissipate, and pure faith and knowing would take its place.

The Cosmic Will

"I Will" comes right at the very center of "I AM," and it is the strongest expression of the cosmic life force within you. Without "I Will," there is no expression of the "I AM," and no "me" that is created by the will of the I AM. The degree of your willpower manifests in direct proportion to the degree of your belief in it. The greater your belief in your own willpower, the greater the Will that manifests it.

The one who can't, will not. The one who can, will. Stepping out of fear and stepping into faith can be done by a mere shift in mental attitude. With the recognition of the I AM within you and its latent powers, you can find and cultivate a mental attitude that will permanently aid you in shifting fear and worry into confidence and faith, which will inevitably be expressed and manifested as persistent determination and confident expectation. This is done by shifting from the illusions of "I can't," created by the conditioned mind of the "me" or "creation," into the truth of "I CAN AND I WILL," manifested by the Infinite Unconditioned Mind of the Creator as confidence and determination.

Whenever you find yourself particularly lacking the willpower to manifest your will in action, earnestly assert, "I CAN AND I WILL," for by doing so, you call upon the expression of the powers dormant in the infinite "I AM." By staying true to this mental attitude with persistent determination, you are rewarded with its forces upon demand. The greater and longer you hold this mental attitude, the more effortless things will become. You will not only be able to create a prosperous life effortlessly, but you will be in full control of everything with ease.

Effortless Action

Effortless action is manifested firstly by the unlocking of the Cosmic Will through an intense burning desire to commit to concentrating your attention toward a particular aim or goal. Effortless Action is expressed via the subconscious mind and manifests in the lines of least resistance, which is also known as the path that requires the least amount of effort, energy, and opposition.

We have discussed how your will manifests in accordance with your dominant desires. In order to complete the first step of expressing effortless action, your aim must become your dominant desire and rule out the consideration of your other options. You cannot will to do two or three things at once. You only have the present moment, and with that, you can only will to do one thing at a time, and you will to do what you desire the most to do, whether the desire of your will to do is expressed consciously or unconsciously.

Sure, you can do one thing for five minutes, and then another thing for thirty minutes, and then come back and do the original thing for twenty more minutes until you switch off to something else, but by doing so, you will not only weaken your desire to commit, you will also weaken your odds of entering into the state of effortless action by cause of utilizing the effort of your conscious attention in different directions and toward different aims.

The Subconscious Mind manifests Effortless Action. The greater portions of what you do on a daily basis, you do automatically without

Effortless Action

effort and little to no will. Whether it be walking, driving, typing on a keyboard, playing a musical instrument, or any other similar operations regarding muscular movements that you have committed to concentrating on, it has been brought from the conscious to the subconscious, where it is now done automatically as a result of persistent determination and repetition of your will to do the thing habitually. As you continue to direct your attention and concentrate on performing a course of action with repetition, you will find that it becomes easier and easier, and you gradually become less and less conscious of certain details required to perform the action, where you inevitably reach the state of effortless action, and perform the actions effortlessly or with the least amount of conscious effort.

Not only do you do the basic things you do in your everyday life automatically, such as what we mentioned above, but in this way, you also perform your daily tasks effortlessly in the direction of the subconscious. In the same way that you would be required to use your conscious effort and will to perform a new course of action or a new daily task, if you have not yet done so to create prosperity, you will be required to do so, not only once or twice, but every day, persistently, if you wish to reap the benefits of creating prosperity effortlessly.

Therefore, find the infinite willpower buried dormant within you and unlock it through the recognition of "I AM." Cultivate a burning desire to live a life where there is no fear or worry and commit to serving others for the rest of your life. Earnestly assert, "I CAN AND I WILL!"

Effortless Action

Following this section, There are three sets of prompts on the left page that must be answered in the morning and one set of prompts on the right page that must be answered before heading to sleep. The questions on the left side will be the same every day, while the questions on the right will change daily.

You are required to answer these prompts earnestly every day, in the morning and at night. Failure to do so will result in misusing the workbook, and therefore, you will not reap the reward of expressing effortless action. The degree of concentrated attention given to the following prompts, including the degree of concentrated attention given to your aim, determines the degree of the impression you will make upon your subconscious mind, and the greater the degree of the impression you make, the less effort it will require.

On the left-hand side, you will be required to answer the prompts that will aid you with (1) desire and purpose, (2) aim and concentration, and (3) committed determination and confident expectation. Answering these questions appropriately will ensure you're on the right track toward creating a prosperous life according to the path of least resistance. After you fill out the three sets of prompts, I encourage you to continue your days as you have been, aligning yourself with your aim while thinking from your vision. Remember, the greater your degree of concentration toward your aim of prosperity, the easier it will become and the less effort it will take. By ensuring your greatest desire is prosperity, you will not be sidetracked by other desires.

Effortless Action

On the following right-hand page, you will find a set of questions that you will be required to answer before falling asleep at night. You will find that the following questions will differ daily in accordance with the different aspects of thought, emotion, and behavior that I will be targeting. Some exercises will require you to reflect on your day, while others will require you to visualize the future. I find it not necessary to explain in deep detail the reasoning behind the questions I will be asking for the sake of simplicity and to ensure the full effect that will be caused as a result of answering them appropriately. I endeavor to have your mind completely reconditioned into a Wealth Consciousness that will be expressed effortlessly and automatically by the end of the workbook.

If you find that you have not seen any results, then I encourage you to re-read the book and practice all parts and exercises again. Even if you find that you have seen results, whether they be small or major, which is most likely the case, and which case will depend on the state you were in prior to receiving this book, I still encourage you to re-read the book repetitively. Each time you re-read the book, I will ensure that you will gain more wisdom, and as you do, you will be reading the book and identifying new perspectives that may not have been understood or identified the first time you read it.

And now, prepare yourself as the final stage of obtaining Wealth Consciousness awaits. You can be a Master of Wealth and a Master of Self, if you but will to claim it by asserting, "I AM, I CAN, I WILL, I DO!"

Effortless Action
Part 3

How strongly do I desire to create financial
freedom? Why do I desire financial freedom?

_____

_____

_____

What is my definite aim? What will I concentrate on
today to move toward my aim? Will I be sidetracked?

_____

_____

_____

How determined and committed am I to creating
prosperity? Am I moving with faith and confidence?

_____

_____

_____

Effortless Action
Part 3

Visualize your commitment to financial success. What does it look like? How does it feel? Claim it below.

_____

_____

_____

_____

_____

_____

_____

_____

_____

_____

Effortless Action
Part 3

How strongly do I desire to create financial freedom? Why do I desire financial freedom?

_____

_____

_____

What is my aim? What will I concentrate on today to move toward my aim? Will there be sidetracks?

_____

_____

_____

How determined and committed am I to creating prosperity? Am I moving with faith and confidence?

_____

_____

_____

Effortless Action
Part 3

Visualize yourself mastering and executing a skill or hobby. Commit to this skill and claim the master self.

_____

_____

_____

_____

_____

_____

_____

_____

_____

_____

_____

Effortless Action
Part 3

How strongly do I desire to create financial freedom? Why do I desire financial freedom?

_____

_____

_____

What is my aim? What will I concentrate on today to move toward my aim? Will there be sidetracks?

_____

_____

_____

How determined and committed am I to creating prosperity? Am I moving with faith and confidence?

_____

_____

_____

Effortless Action
Part 3

Was today aligned with my aim? Am I concentrating and focusing on my aim? Assert your focus.

_____

_____

_____

_____

_____

_____

_____

_____

_____

_____

_____

Effortless Action
Part 3

How strongly do I desire to create financial freedom? Why do I desire financial freedom?

_____

_____

_____

What is my aim? What will I concentrate on today to move toward my aim? Will there be sidetracks?

_____

_____

_____

How determined and committed am I to creating prosperity? Am I moving with faith and confidence?

_____

_____

_____

Effortless Action
Part 3

Am I living my financial purpose? How am I serving others? What have I done today to move toward it?

Effortless Action
Part 3

How strongly do I desire to create financial freedom? Why do I desire financial freedom?

_____

_____

_____

What is my aim? What will I concentrate on today to move toward my aim? Will there be sidetracks?

_____

_____

_____

How determined and committed am I to creating prosperity? Am I moving with faith and confidence?

_____

_____

_____

Effortless Action
Part 3

What are you learning? How does it feel to have the luxury of time and means? How does it feel to be rich?

_____

_____

_____

_____

_____

_____

_____

_____

_____

_____

_____

Effortless Action

Part 3

How strongly do I desire to create financial
freedom? Why do I desire financial freedom?

_____

_____

_____

What is my aim? What will I concentrate on today to
move toward my aim? Will there be sidetracks?

_____

_____

_____

How determined and committed am I to creating
prosperity? Am I moving with faith and confidence?

_____

_____

_____

Effortless Action
Part 3

Are you controlling your will, or is your will controlling you? Are you consciously creating daily?

_____

_____

_____

_____

_____

_____

_____

_____

_____

_____

_____

Effortless Action
Part 3

How strongly do I desire to create financial freedom? Why do I desire financial freedom?

_____

_____

_____

What is my aim? What will I concentrate on today to move toward my aim? Will there be sidetracks?

_____

_____

_____

How determined and committed am I to creating prosperity? Am I moving with faith and confidence?

_____

_____

_____

Effortless Action
Part 3

You have the freedom of choice.
What are you choosing?

_____

_____

_____

_____

_____

_____

_____

_____

_____

_____

_____

Effortless Action
Part 3

How strongly do I desire to create financial freedom? Why do I desire financial freedom?

_____

_____

_____

What is my aim? What will I concentrate on today to move toward my aim? Will there be sidetracks?

_____

_____

_____

How determined and committed am I to creating prosperity? Am I moving with faith and confidence?

_____

_____

_____

Effortless Action
Part 3

You are in full alignment with your financial success.
Visualize and Claim your life below.

_____

_____

_____

_____

_____

_____

_____

_____

_____

_____

_____

Effortless Action
Part 3

How strongly do I desire to create financial freedom? Why do I desire financial freedom?

_____

_____

_____

What is my aim? What will I concentrate on today to move toward my aim? Will there be sidetracks?

_____

_____

_____

How determined and committed am I to creating prosperity? Am I moving with faith and confidence?

_____

_____

_____

Effortless Action
Part 3

Visualize celebrating financial success with your loved ones. What does it look like? How does it feel? Claim it.

Effortless Action
Part 3

How strongly do I desire to create financial freedom? Why do I desire financial freedom?

_____

_____

_____

What is my aim? What will I concentrate on today to move toward my aim? Will there be sidetracks?

_____

_____

_____

How determined and committed am I to creating prosperity? Am I moving with faith and confidence?

_____

_____

_____

Effortless Action
Part 3

*Where is your energy being directed toward the most?
What are you focusing on? Are you consciously
protecting the garden of your subconscious mind?*

_____

_____

_____

_____

_____

_____

_____

_____

_____

Effortless Action
Part 3

How strongly do I desire to create financial freedom? Why do I desire financial freedom?

_____

_____

_____

What is my aim? What will I concentrate on today to move toward my aim? Will there be sidetracks?

_____

_____

_____

How determined and committed am I to creating prosperity? Am I moving with faith and confidence?

_____

_____

_____

Effortless Action
Part 3

Your cosmic will is taking care of things effortlessly.
Visualize and feel it to be true. How does it feel?

Effortless Action
Part 3

How strongly do I desire to create financial freedom? Why do I desire financial freedom?

_____

_____

_____

What is my aim? What will I concentrate on today to move toward my aim? Will there be sidetracks?

_____

_____

_____

How determined and committed am I to creating prosperity? Am I moving with faith and confidence?

_____

_____

_____

Effortless Action
Part 3

Describe your daily routine. What does it look like?
Are you in full alignment with your aim? Claim it.

_____

_____

_____

_____

_____

_____

_____

_____

_____

Effortless Action
Part 3

How strongly do I desire to create financial freedom? Why do I desire financial freedom?

_____

_____

_____

What is my aim? What will I concentrate on today to move toward my aim? Will there be sidetracks?

_____

_____

_____

How determined and committed am I to creating prosperity? Am I moving with faith and confidence?

_____

_____

_____

Effortless Action
Part 3

What challenges have you recently faced? How can you overcome them? Visualize yourself overcoming your challenges with ease.

_____

_____

_____

_____

_____

_____

_____

_____

_____

Effortless Action
Part 3

How strongly do I desire to create financial freedom? Why do I desire financial freedom?

_____

_____

_____

What is my aim? What will I concentrate on today to move toward my aim? Will there be sidetracks?

_____

_____

_____

How determined and committed am I to creating prosperity? Am I moving with faith and confidence?

_____

_____

_____

Effortless Action
Part 3

What skills are you cultivating and mastering? Are these skills going to bring value to others? Visualize yourself mastering your skills and getting paid for it.

Effortless Action
Part 3

How strongly do I desire to create financial freedom? Why do I desire financial freedom?

_____

_____

_____

What is my aim? What will I concentrate on today to move toward my aim? Will there be sidetracks?

_____

_____

_____

How determined and committed am I to creating prosperity? Am I moving with faith and confidence?

_____

_____

_____

Effortless Action
Part 3

How does it feel to be wealthy in consciousness? How does it feel knowing you're already rich? Celebrate your success. It is finished.

_____

_____

_____

_____

_____

_____

_____

_____

_____

_____

Capabilities

What value can I offer?

What skills do I have experience in?

What am I good at doing and teaching?

I AM COMPLETE